# God's Dinosaurs

## *A Biblical Study*

by
Allen E. Nance, Jr.

PublishAmerica
Baltimore

© 2010 by Allen E. Nance, Jr.
All rights reserved. No part of this book may be reproduced, stored in a retrieval system or transmitted in any form or by any means without the prior written permission of the publishers, except by a reviewer who may quote brief passages in a review to be printed in a newspaper, magazine or journal.

First printing

PublishAmerica has allowed this work to remain exactly as the author intended, verbatim, without editorial input.

Softcover 978-1-60836-884-6
PAperback 978-1-4512-5152-4
PUBLISHED BY PUBLISHAMERICA, LLLP
www.publishamerica.com
Baltimore

Printed in the United States of America

# God's Dinosaurs

*A Biblical Study*

# Preface

More often than not people who are doing research on a familiar topic will look up what others have said on the subject then just put their words together in a different order. The ultimate result is their research simply restates what has already been stated. That type of research does not leave one's mind open to new concepts. It is probably most comforting to the researcher to realize that what they believe is supported by the opinions of those that came before them.

In an effort to avoid this type of repetitive information conveyance, I will not quote any non-biblical source in this work. I do consult various resources because it is important to relate new information to what we have been previously taught. In doing so I make a concerted effort not to plagiarize any source or quote any author. However, since the topic of my research is biblically based I will quote verses from the Bible. The Bible is also the primary source to which I would like my readers to refer.

If a reader has the desire or need to verify any of the biblical or non-biblical information included in my work it is their prerogative to use any research resources they choose. It is my hope they will use the Bible as their first and primary resource.

Even using the works of others from other resources that have a biblical context will usually just reconfirm what we have been taught for many years. No new information will be added.

I know this all sounds contradictory since I obviously want readers to use my work as a source of information. I do, however, recommend the reader have their Bible handy as they read to read and verify any verses or passages I reference. I would hope the reader would use my work as a guide to read the Bible as it is written as opposed to how it is often taught. This book is not to be taken as the Word of God. It should be used as a guide to correctly read and understand God's Word in regard to this topic. Prayerfully within this text the reader will find new information. That is, information that is different from what has been traditionally taught.

It is God's desire that we as believers get back to teaching and living His word as He had man to record it. Currently we teach it as man has interpreted it based on what he wants it to be. In Matthew 28: 20 Jesus tells us to teach believers "to observe all things whatsoever I have commanded you…" Effectively teaching God's Word, as it is written, is one way this commandment will be accomplished. Jesus did teach from and say we should know the scriptures. (John 5:39) Of course, the scriptures He referred to are the words we today call the Old Testament. The first book of these very scriptures is what I hope to guide you through as if you are reading it with a previously uninfluenced mind.

If you choose to research further what I have written, use the Bible, as it is written, as your primary resource. If another resource or common teaching conflicts with God's Word, choose the one you feel is the truth.

# Why Is the Study Needed?

A Christian child was upset because another child, who may or may not have been a Christian, asked him a question he could not answer. Because the theory of evolution is taught exclusively in schools today, it was a question the Christian child had in the back of his own mind but was afraid to ask. **What does the Bible say about the existence of dinosaurs?** I can remember having that very question in my mind as a child. We would go to church on Sunday and hear that God spoke the animals into existence and formed man from the ground. It was my understanding from the preacher that these same animals were taken onto the ark and would eventually repopulate the Earth. I remember thinking then that the same animals God created in the beginning are the same animals on the Earth today. Then Monday through Friday we went to school and were taught about evolution. Life began by accident then over the course of millions upon millions of years dinosaurs developed and died off. Then modern animals and humans developed. I believed what the preacher said, but because I liked science I wanted to believe what the teachers taught also. The teachers were helped by the fact that large bones had been found that belonged to these animals we call dinosaurs.

The teachers taught from the text books. The preacher taught from the Bible. I was too young at that time to realize how wrong the theory of evolution had to be. So, although I never asked, I wondered within. I know what the science book says about the existence of dinosaurs, but '**What does the Bible say about the existence of dinosaurs?'**

As an adult I have come to realize, through conversations with other adults, that, I would venture to say, most Christians have had the same question in their mind. Despite that fact, this is a question that the majority of religious leaders would rather ignore or avoid than address. They probably avoid the conversation because the topic was not addressed in their theological education. Just as Darwin's theory of evolution does not leave room for God, conventional religious education and teaching does not leave room for the dinosaurs. A typical religious response to the question might be, "There are mysteries of life that the Bible does not answer, but the Bible gives us all the knowledge we need for our faith." That's just a fancy way of saying, "I don't know." That very type of evasive answer is what gives the scientific community of Darwinism the ability to label religion as merely a 'human psychological need' and not the truth. Satan uses the avoidance of the subject of the dinosaurs by the religious community to his advantage. The lack of a direct biblical explanation, along with fossil evidence that dinosaurs once existed, makes it easy to get the people to believe the theory of evolution is the truth. The theory of evolution still being included in science text books, along with the fact that most court decisions are made in Satan's favor also helps his cause. I think it is time for that very crucial question to be answered biblically. A definitive answer, supported by scripture, will remove one more weapon from Satan's arsenal.

Unfortunately the groups of people who are addressing the

issue are mainly scientists who claim to be Christian. The fact they are scientists first skews their explanations towards evolutionary teaching. They start with the theories of science then try to reconcile them with the Bible. To arrive at the truth of this subject it is important to begin with the Bible. It is important to have the truth as your starting point rather than scientific theory.

I think the religious community will agree that the Bible is the truth. The question that needs to be addressed and answered concerning that statement is whether or not the historical portion of the Bible is the complete history of the Earth, as far as is necessary for us to understand the things that are observed in this world. The answer to that question is important to keep man from trying to explain those observations without God, by creating false gods, or through worldly theories. This has been the case throughout the written history of man. Before we had very much knowledge of science, or knowledge of the true God, we created a new god every time something new was observed that did not fall under a category of one of the gods previously created. During the strength years of Judaism and with the rise of Christianity we started to give credit to God. As we expanded our scientific knowledge we then started to explain everything as naturally occurring; no God needed.

The two most commonly known creative scientific explanations for the existence of the world and life are the Big Bang and Primordial Soup theories. These theories state all of the matter of the universe was contained in one ball until it exploded in a 'Big Bang'. Then in time (billions of years) two non-living amino acids, just by chance, bumped into each other in a pool of water, joined, and became the first component of life, a protein; and all of life as we know it developed from that point in time. I may be simplifying things a bit, but it would seem to take more faith to believe these two scenarios could have produced the great diversity of life on earth than to believe the truth that is written in the Bible: God created the heavens and the earth. It all comes down to where you put your faith. Even with the evidence that the dinosaurs once existed I choose to put my faith in God and His written word. Believers in God must conclude that the origin of the physical universe was at God's hand, not an uncontrolled big bang. The origin of life was at God's discretion and direction, not by accident in a primordial soup pond.

Another theory that has been discussed among scientists concerning the existence of life is spontaneous generation. There have actually been experiments conducted to try to show that, under the right circumstances, life can be produced from none living matter without God. Of course they have not been successful, but that shows how desperately evolutionists want to be right.

Bones of animals that no longer exist have been observed in this earth. That fact can not be ignored. Science has explained their existence without God. They call it evolution. While most religious teachers will deny that the scientific claim of evolution is the truth, they will avoid offering another explanation that would directly address the existence of these extinct animals. In recent years some religious leaders have actually given in to Satan's influence and made statements that both evolution and religious explanations could be true. That is one more reason that there needs to be an explanation for the existence of these bones that includes God and His act of creation as recorded in His Word. Anyone who truly has faith that the Bible is the truth must therefore ask the question, "Is the existence of these animals recorded in God's Word?" We, as believers, must be able to include God in the explanation of every phenomenon we observe. We must be able to include God in the explanation of these extinct animals. In order to do that effectively any viable religious explanation must be based on God's written Word. That is the only way to combat Satan and the scientific based explanations.

To answer this important question and show that God's Word does include the discussion of these extinct animals one must think outside of the box. That is not to say think outside of the Word of God. I am saying you need to think outside of traditional religious teaching. The cycle of secular education is to learn from our teachers then continue researching to expand our knowledge. This is especially evident in the scientific community. The typical cycle in Biblical education is that we learn from our teachers and accept what we are taught without question. If it doesn't make sense we are told to accept it on faith. We are also told that just because we don't understand it doesn't mean it is not true because our wisdom is not equal to God's. (Isaiah 55:8 and 1 Corinthians 3:19) When we mature and become teachers ourselves, we simply teach what we were taught and expect our students to accept it without question with the same explanation.

Religious teachers will say the Bible is the truth, but continue to teach only what they have been taught even if it is not what the Bible actually says. That is why, in both Catholic and Protestant churches, we still teach things that were infused into the Christian religion by the Romans. An example of this is the common teaching of the Trinity as God the Father, God the Son, and God the Holy Spirit. (That is a topic for another work.) We must change the typical pattern of religious education and continue to search the Bible for more of what God truly wants us to learn. I believe God does want us to understand. That is why He had His Word written. The previously mentioned verses simple mean we are not able to understand without His Word.

We must learn to read the Bible for what it says and not for what we want it to say. In order to get the full story of what God wants us to know we must read the words that are there and analyze, through prayer and the guidance of the Holy Spirit, what they really tell us (exegesis). Unfortunately we usually hear the stories first then read into the words what we have been taught (eisegesis). That is why the explanation of the dinosaurs is not included in traditional religious teaching. That story has not been told in a religious context. Even after the bones of the dinosaurs were discovered none of the religious teachers felt the need to change the old Bible Stories. No one that I am aware of went back to the Bible for an explanation of these discoveries. Some did, however, make up their own stories. As believers we know the truth of the Bible does not change. Because of that fact, all of these years we have assumed the Bible stories we have been told are accurate to what the Bible says. Therefore, when we read the words we subjectively read into them what we have already been taught. We must learn to objectively read the Bible to receive the true messages God wants us to have.

It is not my intention to change what the Bible says, but rather to correct the creation story to reflect more accurately what the Bible actually says. In doing so I hope to provide the biblical answer to the existence of the dinosaurs and destroy the myths of spontaneous generation, primordial soup, big bang, and evolution of species.

I believe the Bible teaches us that we should learn from our teachers, but our spiritual education should not stop there. Every Christian is encouraged to, "*Study to shew thyself approved unto God, a workman that needeth not to be ashamed, rightly dividing the word of truth.*" (2 Timothy 2:15) Each person must continue to study God's Word for their self; past what we have been taught. Our studying will be successful if we allow ourselves to be led by the Holy Spirit and our minds to be open to the wisdom of God's Word. We must go beyond simply having knowledge of the words that are printed and the stories we have been told. We must be receptive to the wisdom that the words contain. 1 Corinthians 12:8 tells us, *"For to one is given by the Spirit the word of wisdom; to another the word of knowledge by the same Spirit."* We tend to accept the word of knowledge but not necessarily seek the word of wisdom. The wisdom of man is not enough to bring religion and science together on this subject. We must allow the wisdom of the Holy Spirit to help us rightly divide the word of truth. That is how, as a people, our knowledge of the truth that God's word reveals will grow from generation to generation. The truth that God's Word reveals on this subject is that the dinosaurs were a part of his creation and they are mentioned in the Bible.

As should be expected, the particular book we will be primarily concerned with for this discussion is the book of Genesis. A thorough study of the first two chapters of Genesis will reveal the truth on this subject. There are some religious teachers that will say the first two chapters of Genesis only give us the information we need to know about the creation. There is enough information to establish God as the creator and man as God's choice to have dominion in the world. That is enough of an explanation for most. That same group will also say there are some gaps that can not be, and do not need to be, explained. These statements come mostly from the religious leaders that either will avoid the topic of the origin of the dinosaur altogether, or have assimilated the evolutionary teaching into their religious teaching. The subject is difficult for most Christians because, even though we believe in the Bible, we still have embedded in us the idea of millions of years of evolution that we have been taught in science class from elementary school on. Adding to the difficulty is the fact that throughout our religious upbringing, despite the number of sermons we have heard preached on the subject of creation, the specific subject of the dinosaurs has been ignored. I would revise the earlier religious teachers statement by saying the first two books of Genesis gives us all of the information we need to know about the creation(s).

Another difficulty surfaces when trying to explain the dinosaurs and maintain the traditional religious teaching that Adam and Eve were the first man and woman. That teaching traditionally tells us Adam was created before all of the animals (ch. 2, vs. 18-19). Of course this same traditional teaching also conflicts with the prehistoric human bones that have been discovered. These conflicts do not only present difficulties for Christians teaching Christians, they become a major stumbling block when trying to explain to non-believers that when the Bible says, "In the beginning", it truly means just that. The point in time referred to in that phrase was the beginning of the existence of matter and this physical universe and everything we are able to observe on a physical basis. Science teaches us, in contrast, there was a big bang many millions of years ago. It suggests matter has always existed. It also teaches the dinosaurs lived millions of years before man. Therefore, while discussing the truth of Genesis it is necessary to show both the fallacies of scientific explanations along with the shortcomings of traditional religious teaching.

It is my belief that the historical context of the creation in the book of Genesis is the complete truth. That is, complete to the point that through a thorough knowledge of God's word, and the wisdom and guidance of the Holy Spirit, we are able to understand, to some extent, all things we observe in this world. There are no gaps for the dinosaurs to fall through. The first five books of God's Word were given to Moses at a time when the world worshipped many gods. Some societies of that day created a different god for every phenomenon that was observed but was otherwise unexplainable through human knowledge. We have since done a full 180 degree turn. Our scientific textbooks today are written in a way that teaches we now have enough knowledge to explain everything as naturally occurring; no God needed. God, in His great wisdom and foresight, gave us the Bible so we would have the ability, through study, to know the truth. By knowing the truth we can know first and foremost that He is God. He does not want us making things up to satisfy our ignorance, as we have done in the past. He also does not want us to rely on our own knowledge as the science textbooks teach. Since we have seen evidence of the existence of the dinosaurs, then they must be mentioned in the Word God left for our knowledge and His edification. They are, in fact, mentioned in the Bible in the book of Genesis. We must recognize, and be able to show, God's word is the complete truth and not continue to allow Darwin's ignorant speculation to be taught as the truth. If he had been a Christian maybe he would have searched the Bible for an explanation of his observations and not made unfounded assumptions and speculations.

Man has always had a yearning to understand what we call nature. While attempting to achieve this understanding, we have come up with all types of hypothesis and theories on how things came to be and why things happen the way they do. The theories of the Big Bang and evolution are the most widely accepted explanations. But man, relying on his own understanding of nature, will always have more questions than answers. When he does not have the answers he wants, he will rationalize until he is satisfied. Then, as man's intelligence increases and the answers no longer work, man will adjust or totally change his answers. The truth does not need to be adjusted. Answers that come from the truth will fit even when knowledge increases or situations change. Increased knowledge should serve to increase our understanding of the truth. The source of that knowledge is the key. Moses recorded the truth that was given to him by God. All of the answers are written therein. If man truly wants to understand nature he must read and believe the truth as it is recorded in the Bible. Man can not rely on his own knowledge and wisdom as Darwin and his subsequent followers have done. The Bible tells us the wisdom of man is foolishness to God. (1 Corinthians 3:19) To believe two amino acids bumped into each other and evolved into the dinosaurs and eventually us is foolishness. If we wish to understand nature, we must understand the Word of God.

When scientists are looking for answers they tend to miss the truth they seek because they want their answers to fit their self-proclaimed hypotheses and theories. In affect, they usually have already pre-determined what the answers should be. Often they are not actually seeking the truth, but only trying to prove their hypothesis to be correct. Yes, there is a difference in the two. They also want scientific processes to be necessary in order to find the answers. Therefore scientists' hypothetical and theoretical explanations will ultimately influence how they seek the answers. In some cases they actually devise methods to prove their theories correct. This will be discussed further in the section on radiometric dating.

Scientists do not want the truth to be easy to find, or already known, because they would then have nothing to discover. If they admit the Bible to be the truth, that would only leave them the task of proving the truth. It was a pleasure to find, while I was doing research for this project, that a significant part of the scientific community now realizes increased scientific knowledge does in fact prove the truth of the Bible. Still, most scientists want to be able to discover something new and have a scientific explanation for it, or simply find explanations for existing scientific theories. Noticing that scientists' explanations change every few years, it is easy to see their theories, and the explanations of those theories, must not be the truth.

Because scientists have taught the theory of evolution, with its many revisions, since the time of Darwin, and because it is embedded in everyone who has attended school over the past 150 years, I will spend considerable time discussing the fallacies of that theory. Dispelling evolution is necessary when discussing the truth.

While making the statement that pre-historic life evolved and died off then modern life evolved, scientists speculate it would have taken millions upon millions of years for these things to have occurred. They then devised a method to show how many millions of years old the dinosaur bones must be. Notice I did not say they devised a method to find the age of the dinosaur bones. This method that would show millions of years is called radiometric dating. Scientists claim to know how long it takes for radioactive materials to decay back to non-radioactive materials. By measuring the amount of radioactive materials in organic materials, they claim to be able to tell its age. As I have already stated, this will be discussed in more detail later. This is just one example of how scientists first developed a theory then tried to prove their theory (millions of years) rather than search for the truth. I will show how this practice of radiometric dating could not possibly be considered accurate.

Before scientists, who claim to be Christian, could make the statement of the earth being here for millions of years they had a hurdle to cross. The Bible describes the creation of the earth and its inhabitants in terms of days, not eons. In order to get around that hurdle and not have to cross it they do not object to the use of the word day. They simply say the days in Genesis 1 are not twenty-four hour days. Although the Bible measures the days by the evening and the morning, scientists explain each day as representing an era. Because they want the history of the Earth to have taken millions of years, they will honor evolutionary scientists and change the truth into a lie (Romans 1:25). These are scientists who will say they believe in an almighty God then in the next statement will say it would have taken billions of years for the universe to have been formed and reach its current state. They forget they are talking about God's power to create.

This same group will first say they are Christian but will explain everything from a scientific view point. The Bible says God created the heavens and the earth. These people claim to believe that and at the same time say the early earth was not fit for man to inhabit it for billions of years after God created it. Isaiah 45:18 tells us, "…*He formed it to be inhabited…*" Once again they put science before God, forgetting God created the very laws of science they try to use to justify their billions of years theory. They limit God's power. One person actually went as far as saying God works in this world through natural processes. This puts the processes before God. Once again he forgot the fact that God created those very processes.

I think the primary problem is that as we become more educated we forget the source of true knowledge and wisdom. Colossians 2:2-3 tells us, *"That their hearts might be comforted, being knit together in love, and unto all riches of the full assurance of understanding, to the acknowledgement of the mystery of God, both of the Father, and of Christ; In whom are hid all the treasures of wisdom and knowledge."* We begin to think the knowledge we get from text books and professors is the ultimate knowledge. We place our worldly education ahead of our Christian education. We put our text books before the Bible.

One author that I read had credentials of a master's degree in Theological Studies and a doctorate in Christian Education. Yet, when discussing the book of Genesis he reconciled everything to what he learned in his science classes. He interpreted everything to fit the 'millions of years' evolutionary theories. The six creation days became six geological or cosmological ages. He used the statement that dinosaurs lived millions of years before man to deny the six days could have been literal days. Although he described himself as a preacher rather than a scholar, his words were that of a scholar first. I would go as far as to call him a worldly scholar.

I do not intend to address all of the statements he made that I feel are theologically contradictory. I could write a book about his book. I just wanted to show how much influence our secular education has on how we interpret the scriptures. If we continue to receive traditional religious education that does not explain everything we observe in this world we look for education elsewhere. When we feel we are more educated than everyone else, it seems we stop consulting the Holy Spirit for guidance as we read. We think we can figure it out by ourselves.

The Bible has not changed since it was written. (The exception to this is the books the Catholic Church added to the Old Testament.) The truth does not change. Therefore I will use the truth of the Bible to explain the existence of the dinosaurs. I may use some facts of nature that may be termed scientific, but they will be used only to support the facts of the Bible. I will, in fact, show that neither the scientific theory of evolution nor the practice of radiometric dating could possibly reveal the truth. We only need to thoroughly read God's Word with the guidance of the Holy Spirit.

# What Do Traditionalists Teach?

When I use the term traditionalist I am referring to all religious teachers who proclaim Adam and Eve to be the first man and woman. I want to make that distinction because there are many interpretations of the Word of God including those that have allowed evolution to creep in. When discussing the book of Genesis different denominations will read the same words but yet have differences in what they teach. Sometimes these differences will show up within the same denomination; from one teacher to another. Because of what I will show later in this discussion of the Bible and the dinosaurs, I don't want those small differences to come into play. Most Christian and Jewish teachers teach Adam to be the first man and Eve to be the first woman. I do not believe the Bible tells us that is the case. However, that is what is traditionally taught. Everyone who teaches this falls into the category of those I call traditionalists. That would include almost all Christian teachers.

There are some creationists who have attempted to explain the dinosaur's existence within the traditional biblical education. While there are a few differences, the majority of them maintain the idea that all animals, including the dinosaurs, were created at the same time. They all refer to day six of the creation. Then there are those who teach the dinosaurs lived and died before modern man and modern animals. The differences between the traditionalists seem to come from how much, and what kind of, influence the many years of secular evolutionary teaching has had on the person. They all seem to include it in their explanations to some degree. The primary differences usually are seen in their explanations of when the dinosaurs died. The former are usually influenced by the natural selection concept. To them the dinosaur's extinction happened after the flood. The later have been influenced by the millions-of-years of evolution idea.

The most common traditionalist explanation is that the dinosaurs were taken onto the Ark with all of the other animals. While trying to make this explanation believable part of the evolutionary teaching called natural selection (survival of the fittest) is often used to explain why they died after leaving the Ark. This group of teachers will sometimes unknowingly include the natural selection reasoning by saying the environment had been changed by the flood. This change would have greatly reduced, or eliminated the food source of the dinosaur. Without their source of food they naturally died off.

There are a couple of problems with this explanation. First and foremost they are leaving God out of the survival portion of the equation. If God had chosen for them to survive He would have provided what they needed. The Bible tells us that God feeds the animals. *"Consider the ravens; for they neither sow nor reap; which neither have storehouse nor barn; and God feedeth them: how much more are ye better than the fowls?"* (Luke 12:24) This verse can be extended to all of God's animals. If the dinosaurs had been on the ark that would have meant God wanted them saved. Only those that were to be saved were taken onto the ark. God would have provided for their needs after leaving the ark. Even if some of the dinosaur species would have become extinct between then and now, some of them would still be around. This explanation is an example of how, even though we deny evolution as being the truth, we are subconsciously still influenced by the years of grade school science classes. The religious teachers who teach this may not even realize they have interjected secular education into biblical explanations.

While some species do become extinct because of environmental changes and other factors, it is not likely every dinosaur species would have died off. Some of them would have been able to survive. If the scientists were correct in their assessment of the dinosaur's diet, the meat eaters would still have had plenty of food as the other animal species re-populated the earth. Even if the dinosaurs and modern animals lived in different areas before the flood, they would have co-existed, that is lived in the same areas, after the flood. The more docile animals we see today would have become the prey for the larger carnivorous dinosaurs. We would be still living with T-Rex today. (I do not believe scientists are correct about when or how the dinosaurs died.)

All vegetation was not destroyed in the flood. If it had been the dove would not have been able to bring the olive leaf back to Noah after the rain had stopped. Even through secondary succession (re-growth after a natural disaster) the olive plant would not have re-grown that quickly. Over time, through secondary succession, the plants that were not able to survive the flood would have been replaced. If that was not true the modern animals would not have been able to survive either. The animals which are lower on the food chain (just above the producers) would have died off first. A chain reaction would have followed. There would have been no long term survivors. Therefore, the herbivores would also have had food for survival. God would have provided for their needs also.

If science (natural selection; survival of the fittest) was the deciding factor, why would the dinosaurs have been less capable of adapting than the modern animals? They would have both been facing the same new environment. You can see here the after flood explanation doesn't work unless you leave God out. Actually it doesn't work even with natural selection thrown in. What I find really funny is that if the modern animals were able to out-compete the dinosaurs then those huge mean beasts, as portrayed by scientist's descriptions and film, were actually pretty wimpy.

From the last paragraph the second objection to the after flood explanation should be obvious. If the environment had changed to the point of causing the extinction of every dinosaur species then the other animal species would have been affected also. They all would have disembarked into an environment that was different from when they went in. Natural selection should have had just as devastating an affect on all of the animals. Also, if the environmental impact was that great how much would Noah's family have been affected? Would man have been able to survive?

Of course we know the humans (Noah's family and descendants) survived because God chose them for survival. That is why we are still here today. The same is true for all of the animals that were taken aboard the ark. God chose the animals that were to survive and He brought them to the ark. God provided for man and animal after the flood. Can any traditional teacher demonstrate a biblical basis for extending God's grace and protection to man and some of the animals but not all? Since none of the dinosaurs have survived, it is apparent God did not choose them for survival, therefore they were not on the ark. It will be discussed in more detail later, but the dinosaurs were actually selected by God to be destroyed in the flood along with all of the other creatures.

Some of the traditionalists who wish to defend this after-flood explanation will say God stepped in after the flood to provide only for the animals that would survive. Since I have just stated that God feeds the animals I will agree with that. Still, if you are saying this is why the dinosaurs died after leaving the ark you are still contradicting God's word. The Bible clearly tells us God took the animals that were chosen for survival to the ark. He would not have taken them aboard the ark then allowed them, as a whole, to die. But, even if you wanted to continue to defend the after flood death of the dinosaurs that means God still made a distinction between the two groups of animals and it was by His decision which group survived. By this logic which comes through faith in God's word, natural selection is shown once again not to have been the mechanism of nature that caused the extinction of the dinosaur. I find it troubling that any Christian would attempt to give what they feel is a biblical explanation for life and include this particular evolutionary component in their explanation.

The basic premise of the after flood explanation is that the Bible says some of all of the animals were taken aboard the Ark. The assumption that is made is that the term 'all' means all of the animals that every existed. Since Moses was writing in a historical context, 'all' most likely meant all of the animals that were on Earth at the time the texts were written. Remember again that God took aboard the ark only those that would be saved. Since the dinosaurs were not saved, they were not taken aboard the ark. All of the animals that were on the Earth at the time of Moses had an ancestor on the ark.

Another assertion this group of traditionalists make is that there was no death on the earth before Adam and Eve's sin. Since it is traditionally taught they (Adam and Eve) were the first humans, it would have been possible for there to have been no death before they ate of the forbidden fruit. There could simply have not been enough time for any creature to have died by natural causes. This is important because I will show later why I do not believe they were the first humans on the Earth. I also believe there was death by both natural and unnatural causes before Adam.

This discussion of pre-Adam death is important because, while I by no means subscribe to the millions-of-years theories of evolution, I do believe there was a period of time between the creation of the living creatures of Genesis chapter one and the formation of Adam in chapter two. I will give the detailed biblical explanation of my belief in the section on what the Bible teaches. All of this fits into the discovery of the dinosaurs in the Bible. Just as the dinosaurs are separated from modern animals so is prehistoric man separated from modern man.

Traditionalists usually make this no-death statement to combat the millions-of-years teachers. Their primary purpose is the show that if dinosaurs had lived millions of years before man and modern animals and became extinct, death would have been on the earth before God told Adam he would surely die. In order to show there was no death before what is commonly called the original sin certain biblical verses are often named. From my reading, none of the named verses say there was no physical death before Adam. They have simply been interpreted to mean that by those who want to continue traditional teaching.

As we discuss these verses there needs to be a distinction made between physical death and spiritual death. We must realize, first, that they are distinctly different. Physical has to do with the temporal; spiritual has to do with the eternal. Some writers interchange the two. I don't know if they do it unknowingly or deliberately. We must be sure we are applying the word death in the correct context and toward the correct creatures.

One of the verses that are mentioned often is Romans 5:12.

"*Therefore, just as through one man sin entered the world, and death through sin, and thus death spread to all men, because all sinned...*" This verse refers to death being brought upon man. It does not say anything about the animals. Furthermore, this verse refers to spiritual death, not physical death. If you continue reading Paul talks about the gift of life that is given through faith in Jesus. Romans 5:18 reads, "*Therefore, as through one man's offense judgment come to all men, resulting in condemnation, even so through on Man's righteous act the free gift came to all men, resulting in justification of life.*" Through Jesus we who believe receive life. Yet, we still dye physically. Those who have faith in Jesus no longer will have death spiritually. They have life.

Some will argue that the death brought upon us through Adam is both spiritual and physical death. It could very well refer to physical death as well. I will discuss in detail later why I do not believe Adam to be the first man. I believe the Bible tells us there were humans (Neanderthal, Cro-Magnon) created before Adam. Therefore our (modern man) physical death would have begun with Adam. Since only modern man, through Noah's family, survived the flood, Romans 5:12 would still be accurate even if applied toward our physical death as well as our spiritual death. Since we are all descendants of Adam through Noah, death was brought upon us by Adam. This still does not mean there was absolutely no physical death by natural or other causes before Adam's sin. The prehistoric men and creatures would have experienced death.

In the same context 1 Corinthians 15:21-22 is often named to show death entered the world because of Adam's sin. "*For since by man came death, by Man also came the resurrection of the dead. For as in Adam all die, even so in Christ all shall be made alive.*" Again, these verses are referring to spiritual death and life. Some say they refer to both physical and spiritual. I disagree. Adam had the Spirit of God in him by His breath. The sin of disobedience in the eating of the fruit both made Adam mortal and killed that Spirit. We once again receive that Spirit through our belief and faith in Christ Jesus. By our faith the Spirit gives us eternal life. Since we still die physically, the death referred to in theses verses that was brought on us by Adam and was overcome by Jesus has to be spiritual death. If these verses referred to physical death all true believers would become immortal. If Jesus' resurrection overcame physical death we would no longer die. The Bible says that flesh and blood shall not enter heaven (1 Corinthians 15:50). Therefore, this physical body which experiences death is not the body which will be made alive through Christ.

Even if a person can not see the difference between physical and spiritual life, it still should be easy to see the passages just mentioned say nothing about animal death before or since Adam's sin. They only refer to man's death. Of the other verses that are often used to justify saying there was no animal death before Adam's sin; none of them actually say that. Genesis 2:17 says eating of the fruit would cause Adam's death. Genesis 1:29-30 tells what God gave the creatures for food. Neither does Romans 8:20-22 talk about animal death. Verses about remission of sin by blood, no more death in the new earth, restitution by Jesus, animals that are now prey and predator lying down together, along with other topics about restoration of God's kingdom, are used to make their case. None of these verses say there was no death by natural causes before Adam's sin. This is what has always been taught so it is simply repeated with verses taken out of context in an attempt to justify the teaching

The traditionalists who would have you to believe that dinosaur and man did not live together are the most puzzling to me. They still want Adam and Eve to be the first man and woman and teach, as all traditionalists do, that the man (male and female) created on the second half of day six are those two. They also teach that all land animals were created on the first half of day six. But, they want the first half of day six to be millions of years before the second half. In general they want both Creationism and Evolution to be true. Of course just to infer the word day could mean millions of years contradicts the Bible. They use a lot of word play to explain and justify their teaching. If you accept their point of view, by the time you have six days of millions of years you now have the billions of years the evolutionaries teach.

The previously discussed group unknowingly included evolutionary components in their explanation. This group, however, deliberately incorporates evolution into biblical teaching. In fact they embrace evolution and don't feel there is anything wrong with combining creationism with evolution. Usually these people are scientists first and Christians second. They may, however, say otherwise in order to get Christians to consider their explanation. With the majority of the population having received the secular education in science, making the word day mean eras of millions of years is convenient. There is no need to make a choice between evolution and creation.

The primary foundation for their explanation is that the word day, in chapter one of Genesis, does not necessarily have to refer to a twenty-four hour day. They make this claim despite the fact that the Bible clearly defines the days in Chapter one of Genesis as the evening and the morning. This is a perfect example of reading into the text what you want it to say. After being taught for years about evolution and believing it, they say God could have used evolution to develop the earth. With that rationale they feel justified in saying a day could really mean an age. That is, a geological age. They wish to limit God's power to satisfy their theory. There are no biblical passages to support this theory. There are, however, extra-Genesis verses that support the six days as literal days. Exodus 20:11 is one such verse. *"For in six days* the Lord made the heavens and the earth, the sea, and all that is in them, and rested the seventh day."

At the time Moses wrote Exodus, at God's direction, all of the events of Genesis where already history. If the days were meant to be taken as ages that is what God would have given him to write. To say otherwise is saying God did not communicate what he meant. God gave the Word to Moses to write it down so we would know the truth. Allowing our imaginations to create is how the Greco Roman myths came to be. That is also how the theory of evolution came to be. Because God had chosen the Hebrew people as His people, He wanted them to have the truth in a written format so there would be no embellishment. Traditionalists who have accepted evolution are trying to embellish what has been written.

There is another group of traditionalists who wish to acknowledge the millions-of-years theories but not have to account for them in the Bible. These teachers usually will claim to believe what is commonly called the "Gap Theory." The way it was explained to me is that the millions of years fell between Genesis 1:1 and Genesis 1:2. The claim is God created everything in verse one. The earth, with the dinosaurs, existed for millions of years then for some unwritten reason was destroyed. In verse two God was starting all over again. This makes absolutely no sense because if the earth was destroyed to the point it had to be reformed there would be no evidence of the dinosaurs for us to find. However, because religious leaders who are looked up to are teaching this I will discuss it and show more of its fallacies.

Even with this group claiming there was an Earth before This Earth we know, I still see this group as traditionalists. Their claim of complete destruction of the first Earth makes verse two a new beginning. They still teach Adam was the first man of the new

Earth. In other words, they want to keep the same stories. They simply created a new preface at the beginning.

Just as with other non-biblical theories the first step in trying to justify the 'gap' is to change the wording of the Bible. The first phrase in Genesis 1:2 reads, "*And the earth was without form and void...*" The Gap Theorists want the word 'was' changed to 'became'. The say the Hebrew word that is used in that place could be interpreted as became. That allows them to state that when God created the Earth in verse one it was complete and inhabited by the dinosaurs. That first earth existed for millions of years. Then for some reason, that God chose not to reveal to us, it was all destroyed. The question that immediately comes to my mind when I listen to this explanation is why would God have destroyed the light? In verse three He had to re-create light if you believe their theory. He also would be re-creating the sun, moon and stars in later verses. Was the entire universe destroyed? Or, did the dinosaurs live in total darkness?

If any good religious teacher wants to be taken seriously and believed he/she must support their teaching with scripture. That is the very reason I quote the Bible as much as is necessary to make my point clear. The same is true for those that teach the gap theory. There are certain verses that are used in their effort to support what they believe. Since there is no direct biblical description of the gap, certain verses are said to 'refer' to the gap. As I read these verses it seems some creative interpretations had to be employed before the references could be made. As we often do, they hold on tightly to what they believe and read into the verses what they want them to say. I don't think any of the verses actually make reference to a previous earth.

One passage that is used is taken from Ezekiel 28:12-15. For some reason gap teachers say the "Eden" mentioned in verse 13 does not refer to the same garden Adam and Eve inhabited. It is clear, when read in context, the message in the passage is directed to the spirit of Satan. With the common belief that the fall of Lucifer came before the formation of Adam and subsequently Eden, it is rationalized this must refer to an earlier Eden. I don't understand why they feel it has to be a different Eden. If Lucifer's fall came before Eden, that would make him available to be present in Eden. We know his spirit was there in the form of the serpent to deceive Eve. Gap teachers have simply decided what they want the passage to mean and the read that into the verses. (Isaiah 14:12-15 is also used when discussing Lucifer's fall.)

Isaiah 45:18 reads, *"For thus saith the Lord that created the heavens; God Himself that formed the earth and made it; He hath established it; He created it not in vain, He formed it to be inhabited; I am the Lord; and there is none else."* This verse is contrasted by the Gap teachers to Genesis 1:2. In doing so the words 'in vain' are translated 'empty or a waste'. By doing so they say the first created earth could not be the one describe in Genesis. *"And the earth was without form, and void...* The explanation given is that the first earth was created fully inhabited. There would not have been a void period as at the beginning of verse 1:2. That is how they would have us to interpret the words 'not in vain'; or 'not empty' or 'not a waste'. They have taken one verse and compared it to the beginning of another verse in order to justify their statement. More to the point they have taken a few words from one verse and compare them to a few words of another verse.

What they miss is the interpretation of the word 'created' in the Isaiah verse mentioned. When discussing what God created, the entire process must be included, not just the initial point of matter being brought into existence. The single act of creating matter would involve only verse 1:1. The creation of the earth encompasses the entire six days, not just the beginning. As stated earlier, Exodus 20:11 makes that clear. God formed the earth to be inhabited. When the creation was complete, all six days, it was inhabited. It was not created in vain. Therefore, Isaiah 45:18 could (does) refer to the creation as described in Genesis chapter 1, not the creation of an unwritten previous earth.

Although there are other verses used when trying to prove their theory, the last verses I will discuss, that gap theorists quote, are Jeremiah 4:23-28. These verses are also quoted as evidence of the destruction of a previous earth. They have taken these verses out of context to try to support their theory. These verse are actually a part of the warning from God to Judah of the destruction that was coming to them. The particular verses mentioned are God's words where He is reminding Judah who He is and of His power. The entire passage, or conversation, has nothing to do with a previous earth.

There are probably many other theories out there. If the description of each theory is not directly found in the Bible it should not be seen as biblical. If verses are chosen from various places and can not be found in one place, the theory is most likely fictitious. God does not want us making up stories then claiming them to be acts of God. If this or any other theory was the truth we would not have to pick and choose verses, and take them out of context, in an attempt to prove the theory. That is the very reason that as I expose the truth I ask you to read the verses that are written in contest and in the order they are written. I do not simply pick and choose a few verses that I think might support something that was just creative thinking to begin with. Read the Bible in context with an open mind and see where it leads you.

# What About Non-Traditionalists?

For the purpose of this work I would identify everyone who can except that Adam and Eve were not the first humans as non-traditionalists. That would include myself. Within the category there is a group of scientists who fully hold to the Big Bang theory while claiming to believe also in creationism. I am not in that group. These scientists do usually limit their evolutionary teaching to the development of the universe and earth. They simply exclude the teaching that life developed through evolution. They have come to realize, through scientific discovery, that the universe had a beginning and therefore a creator. However, because they can not let go of their years of secular science education they still teach there was a big bang event. The difference; they now say God caused the big bang.

The primary faults I find in their explanations are the ways they limit God's power. They in general tend to state that God only starts processes then allows the processes to evolve. God caused all matter to come into existence at the time of the big bang. He then left it alone for many billions of years so the cosmos could form on its own. They say God formed the earth but it took another few million or billion years for it to be habitable by life. God created light on day one. But, it took millions upon millions of years from day one to day three for the sun to form. In short, they do not take the word 'created' literally until you reach the point of the creation of life. To them the first few days of the Bible are to taken as cosmological ages. God only created matter. The universe created its self.

They switch gears on the days when life was created. These days are to be seen as shorter geological ages. These days do not have to be as long because God Created life fully formed. Finally realizing there is no true evidence to support the evolution of life, these scientists choose to take literally the statements of the Bible that God created the living organisms fully formed. They still do not take the term day, even during the creation of life, to mean a twenty-four hour period. Some of them teach that prehistoric men were the ones created by God. It then took tens of thousands of years for them to develop, not evolve, into modern man. Half of the non-traditionalists believe dinosaur and man lived together. I will call them 'Group A. The other half, 'Group B', still believe the dinosaur lived millions of years before man. This group is probably the larger of the two groups. Some of them will actually say the Bible does not mention the dinosaur at all. That is their way of justifying the time frame.

Non-traditionalists pick and choose which parts of scripture to take literally and which not to take literally. Because the true fossil record shows scientifically there could not have been any evolution of life, they take the creation of life as a literal event. Because science has yet to prove the universe did not evolve, they choose to stay with scientific theory concerning time frames. They often put science before scripture.

The one thing Group A teaches that I agree with (but in a

different form) is that dinosaur and man lived together. Some of them teach, as traditionalists do, that all land animals and man were created on day six of Genesis. The Bible clearly says land animals were created on the first half of day six (Gen. 1:24-25). The natural assumption, or rationalization, is that since the dinosaur was a land animal it must have been created on day six. Since the cow and the horse are also land animals they must have also been created on day six. They teach that all land animals, the dinosaurs as well as the animals we see today, were created together. I guess that means they also lived together. One problem with that explanation is that there were also flying dinosaurs that would have been created on day five. Also, this group generally teaches the humans created on day six are not Adam and Eve. These humans were the Cro-Magnon people. They, over time, developed into modern man, Adam and Eve, passing through the Neanderthal stage along the way.

The greatest separation from myself and Group A is the time frame when they say the dinosaur became extinct. The majority of them teach the dinosaur died after the flood. They teach the environmental changes that occurred as a result of the flood made the Earth un-inhabitable for the dinosaur. As I said earlier that is just a way of taking the salvation of the animals out of God's hand and putting in back to natural selection; an evolutionary process.

The biggest problem I have with most of the non-traditionalists is simply that they look at the discussion of the dinosaur from a scientific view. They generally take their evolutionary education and try to include God or the Bible in it. They don't say life evolved but they keep a lot of the time frames that evolutionary theory teaches. They explain away biblical passages that contradict what they teach. They re-define biblical passages to fit what they want to believe. They take passages out of context to support scientific claims. Their position doesn't seem to me to be that of a believer in God and the Bible who happens to be a scientist. It is more of a scientist who claims to believe in God and the Bible. Let's take a look at more of what group B teaches and my objections to it.

For the most part they still teach the millions-of-years time frame for life on the Earth. The dinosaurs lived over 65 million years ago. Also, the six days of creation were not literal days. Of course this is pure scientific teaching. There is nothing biblical about it. They justify making these statements by saying the Bible does not mention the dinosaur at all. In their effort to justify that statement they say the Bible skips subjects that were not necessary because the information would have been useless to the Israelites back in Old Testament times.

If they were believers first and scientists second they would realize the Bible was not written just for the Israelites of the past. It was written for all believers in the past, present, and future. With that in mind we must remember 2 Timothy 3:16 tells us, *"All scripture is given by inspiration of God, and is profitable for doctrine, for reproof, for correction, for instruction in righteousness."* The Bible can be used to prove (reproof) what is true. If you are looking for the truth of the existence of the dinosaur how can a believer discount the Bible or say it does not mean what it says? When we have questions about things we observe in this world the Bible is the first place we should look for answers. The Bible does not skip any subjects. While the word dinosaur is not used in the Bible, they were the animals created by God on day five (flying dinosaurs) and day six in chapter one of Genesis. The six creation days are literal days distinguished by the "evening and the morning." The time frame of the bible can in no way be interpreted to indicate more than 65 Million years as group B would have you believe.

One writer actually made the claim that the Big Bang theory can be used to support the Bible. He insinuated that without God's input there is no way the universe could have developed in only a few billion years. It is absolutely ludicrous to me that a person could claim to believe in God and in the same breath say it would take Him billions of years to create the universe. This person obviously doesn't know the same God I know. He seems to believe God's power is limited. He says progress is only made by chance chemical reactions. He is just the type of person who puts more faith in man (through science) than he does in God (through the Bible).

To further emphasize these 'group B' people are scientist first they state the scientific claims first even when discussing the origin of life. They say life was not created until the fourth day (fourth eon to them) because the early Earth was inhospitable. (Actually life was created on day three with the plants.) For every believer who knows God specifically created the earth for the purpose of being inhabited by life that statement is ridiculous. Once again the person or people who would make this statement are limiting God's power. They are saying God could not, or did not, make the Earth habitable when He took the formless mass, shaped it, and separated the land and the water. Scientists would have you to believe God did not make the Earth hospitable so they can convince you God's creation still need to evolve. Even those who believe the early Earth was covered with water say it would have taken time for the land to appear. They can then stick their millions-of-years back into the discussion.

The truth is when God separated the land and the water the land was ready to support life. That is why He created the plants on the same day. Scientists would have you believe the Earth was a hot ball that had to take millions of years to cool. Millions of years later chemical reactions would cause water vapor to form. It would then take more millions of years before life would form. Genesis 1:2 says, "*And the earth was without form, and void; and darkness was upon the face of the deep. And the Spirit of God moved upon the waters.*" When God took the formless mass and shaped the Earth water was already present. There was not some strange atmosphere that had to go through multiple chemical reactions over millions of years before water vapor was formed. That is more scientific fiction. Where is the sample of the inhospitable atmosphere that was collected from that ancient Earth?

One of the most convincing arguments scientists use to support the evolution of the universe and their millions-of-years teaching is the speed of light. With the given speed of 186,000 miles per second being accepted as fact they say it would take at least millions of years for the light of the stars to reach the earth. That would mean the light we see from any given star would have left that star millions of years ago. If we were dealing strictly with man's understanding of science that would be an unshakable argument. But you must remember we are really discussing the power of God who created the very science man is trying to understand. When you look at things from that perspective you may remember man's wisdom is not complete. 1 Corinthians 3:18-19 reminds us, "*18Let no man deceive himself. If any man among you seemeth to be wise in this world, let him become a fool, that he may be wise. 19For the wisdom of this world is foolishness with God. For it is written, 'He taketh the wise in their own craftiness'.*" This argument of the scientists is made without consulting Gods Word. That makes it incomplete and therefore foolish.

When we add the Bible into the discussion it will not make sense to the purely scientific minded. God's word tells us He created the light before he created the sun, moon, and stars. Light was created on day one. Genesis 1:3-5 tells us, "*3And God said, 'Let there be light'; and there was light. 4And God saw the light, that it was good;*

*and God divided the light from the darkness.* 5*And God called the light Day, and the darkness He called Night. And the evening and the morning were the first day.*" Because secular education tells us there needs to be an energy source to produce light scientists will tell you this is out of order. It does not make sense to our natural mind that there can be light without a physical source for the light. My question to you is, "*Is any thing too hard for the Lord?...*" (Genesis 18:14) They will say they believe in God but do not totally believe in the Bible. Where do you place your faith?

The real key to this discussion is day four when God created the heavenly bodies. They were created after the creation of the plants. Most importantly, they were created for us to see. Verses 14 through 19 tell us, "14*And God said, Let there be lights in the firmament of the heaven to divide the day from the night; and let them be for signs, and for seasons, and for days, and years.* 15*And let them be for lights in the firmament of the heaven to give light upon the earth; and it was so.* 16*And God made two great lights; the greater light to rule the day, and the lesser light to rule the night; He made the stars also.* 17*And God set them in the firmament of the heaven to give light upon the earth.* 18*And to rule over the day and over the night, and to divide the light from the darkness: and God saw that it was good.* 19*And the evening and the morning were the fourth day.*" If you truly believe the Bible is God's word then its words must have dominion over the words of man's science books. The heavenly bodies, including the stars (vs. 16), were created to be seen from the Earth by the beings that would inhabit it. Because God intended for them be seen and used for signs, seasons, days and years, they would be already visible from Earth at the time they were created. They would definitely have been visible when man was created two days later. That is the statement scientists do not want you to realize. However, that is what the Bible tells us. Therefore, if the scientist's statements of light speed and star distances are accurate we simply have yet to see any of the light that may have originated at the source of the stars; except for our sun of course.

Notice in verse 14 the heavenly bodies were for man to be able to measure time. Days and years were specifically mentioned. Therefore the measure of days from that point is the same as we have today; measured by the appearance of the sun. A believer in the Bible should never say days four through seven are more than 24 hours. Since days one through three are described by the same *"evening and morning"* they also should be recognized as 24 hour days.

In an effort to distract you from the truth some non-traditionalists will try to get you to believe the existence of God and evolution are non-related issues. They wish to have you think that way so you will not question how they limit God's abilities by their theories. In the general sense the initial statement is true. Once you buy into that they will follow up by saying God only started the processes then allowed things to evolve naturally. They would also have you to keep the discussion of evolution from seeming essential in a discussion concerning salvation. Again, that is generally a true statement if you are only discussing what it takes to receive the gift of salvation. However, Satan's plan is that believers would start to discount, alter, or disbelieve parts of God's word. If he can make just one person stumble through confusion or disbelief then it could affect that persons understanding of the need to be saved. Satan is working his plan by trying to get you to buy into any part of evolution. If he can accomplish that in the book of Genesis how much can he stretch it as the remainder of the Bible is read and taught?

Although my views are also non-traditional they are biblically based. I thoroughly disagree with evolution being taught in any form. I believe God, in His infinite power, created everything fully intact. There was no need for processes to complete the formation of something God only began. I also feel it is important to state your disbelief in evolution when having discussions on salvation. If Satan can get you to believe natural forces were in control at the beginning and not God, he can get you to believe you can save yourself through faith in the universe. That is what has led to religious groups that commit suicide as comets pass. Such a person may also believe in books that direct you to put your faith in the universe. We were warned in Romans 1:25 this would happen. "Who changed the truth of God into a lie, and worshipped and served the creature more than the Creator, who is blessed for ever. A-men.

Although these scientists call themselves Christian there are many things they teach that they have to adjust the meanings of the words of the Bible to justify. It seems to me that people who put man's wisdom (science) before God's word is putting their faith in the wrong place. If you are truly a believer you must first show your faith in the Bible then justify you scientific teaching accordingly. If you believe in your secular science education first then try to adjust the Bible to fit you are putting your faith in man.

# What Does the Bible Say?

**Different Creations: The Chronologies of Genesis 1 & 2**

This section is what this work is all about. The previous sections were necessary in order to establish a proper perspective. Before we can recognize what is really truth it is important to see what is being taught from various perspectives. It is then possible to compare and critique the various explanations. This comparison is necessary to be able to filter out the bits of truth (Bible based) from the bits of creative thinking (unsubstantiated fiction). If an idea is to be taken as biblical truth the verse used to support the idea should be able to be read in context. If verses have to be chosen at random throughout the bible you should be suspicious of how they are being used. Remember, even Satan quoted scripture out of context (Matthew 4:6). Any discussion that incorporates a component of evolution would be in the creative thinking category. Here we are going to focus on the truth.

In order to have a biblical explanation of anything we absolutely must read the Bible. This is especially true on this subject of the dinosaurs. Many people have given what they claim to be a biblical explanation of the dinosaurs without actually going back and reading anew the verses that would address the topic. They simply take what they have been taught by others, in both religious and secular education, and try to reconcile it in favor of religion by regurgitating commonly used verses. Carefully reading what the Bible actually says is the most important component in finding the truth. Because of this I have quoted the verses that absolutely must be read when discussing this topic. You will also notice I repeat myself often for the purpose of stressing important points. Emphasis of particular words and their in-context meanings are also important. I recommend you have your Bible present as you read this section so that you may check the accuracy of what I have written.

All verses that are quoted are from the King James translation. I would suggest you be sure to use a Bible that is a translation and not simply an interpretation. The King James Version was translated from the original text for the expressed purpose of having an accurate English translation. A lot of the modern Bible versions have been written for ease of reading or understanding. In doing so, the writers have interpreted certain verses to have a single meaning. Usually that meaning is what they have been taught the verse to have. They accomplish this by changing key words in the verses to establish the wanted meaning. Some interpret entire passages to create the learned Bible stories. Please choose a version that would truly be considered a translation. Individual words can make a huge difference when discussing the truth of God's Word.

I have been taught that when the Bible was originally written the books were not separated into chapters and verses as are currently numbered. The chapter and verse numbers were added by the various translators during the transition period of going from the scroll format to the book. Some may have been added as the translations into various languages were made. I believe some were placed for the purpose of supporting the biblical stories as they were commonly taught. Although the King James translation was translated from the original language for accuracy of the text, the organization was influenced by translations that existed at the time. The numbering of the first two chapters of Genesis, I believe, was based on supporting the traditional one creation teaching. I do not hold to that teaching. With that in mind, it is my contention that the first three verses of chapter two should have been placed at the end of chapter one with chapter two beginning at what we now read as verse four. This change helps to explain what I believe is different than I have ever heard taught.

Chapter two is traditionally taught to be a re-statement and further explanation of chapter one. I believe that not to be the case. I believe chapter two, beginning at verse four, stands alone as a description of God forming living creatures that would be different from His first living creations; those created in chapter one. Most will reject this idea primarily because it doesn't allow for Adam and Eve to be the first humans. We want them to be the first for a primarily egotistic reason. We are their descendants through Noah. If they were made in God's image then we are the image of God. Such a major change in theological teaching would be almost impossible for the religious community to accept after thousands of years of the Adam and Eve teaching. It may be considered by some to be heretical. However, this is where we must begin if we are going to discuss the dinosaurs from a biblical perspective. We must break from traditional religious teaching.

The primary thing that will make this concept difficult for most people to accept is our human ego. The Bible states in chapter one that God created man (male and female) in his own image and likeness (Genesis 1:26-27). "26*And God said, Let us make man in our image, after our likeness;... 27 So God created man in His* *own image, in the image of God created He him; male and female created He them."* We are traditionally taught, exclusively, that Adam and Eve were the first man and woman. We also know that we are all offspring of that couple, by way of the ancestral line of Seth through Noah's family. These three statements coupled together allow us to boast that we are made to look like God. Of course the assumption here is that the words 'image' and 'likeness' mean to look like. Our ego will not allow us to think that either Cro-Magnon or Neanderthal men looked more like God than we do. They would have, after all, been created first if Adam and Eve were not.

Scientists and their artists tell us pre-historic men and modern men have different appearances. Of course that requires our accepting the assertion that the bones being found are in fact pre-historic. More importantly it also depends on our accepting that the drawings we have been shown of pre-historic men for years are accurate. Some scientists today admit the artist's renderings of pre-historic men are not accurate, but are nothing more than the images of the artist's imagination. Despite evolutionary scientist's assertions that some bones being found are of humans (pre-historic man) who lived before us (modern man), the religious community feels we must be the ones to look like God. Religious leaders will say, based on the Adam and Eve explanation, that the scientists must be wrong. I say they are both wrong, at least in part. The first humans were spoken into existence (Gen. Ch. 1) before Adam and Eve were formed (Gen. Ch. 2). Although Adam and Eve were formed differently (not spoken into existence) than the first man they had the same appearance. This is confirmed in Genesis 5:1. *"This is the book of the generations of Adam. In the day that God created man, in the likeness of God made He him."* Even with that said, I do not mean to infer necessarily that we look like God, only that we look the same as the first humans.

The word image does not necessarily have to mean to look like. It could mean to be personally designed according to an idea in the mind of the creator. One of the definitions of the word image is 'a mental picture of something'. We have seen often where an artist renders an image on a canvas or out of clay of an idea he has in his own mind. That would be the artist's own image of that idea. This very concept and ability could have been passed on to us from God. We were, after all, given life (consciousness and cognitive ability) by God's own breath. At least some of our patterns of thought would have come from Him also. God could have been saying (in verse 1:26) He was going to design man how He had pre-determined man to look. The Bible teaches us that those who would be saved were chosen before the foundation of the earth (Ephesians 1:4). That would indicate God had an image of the man He would create before He ever created the earth. When God said in verse 1:26 He was going to make man in His image, He was simply being careful to follow His own pre-designed image of what man would be. Besides, even if the word does mean to look like, who is to say scientist's and artist's renderings of pre-historic man are correct? We could look just like them.

The word 'likeness' has been interpreted in various ways. The importance of this is that it could mean 'to be like', not necessarily 'to look like'. I contend that 'to be like' is the correct interpretation. For us to be made in the likeness of God means we have some of the characteristics of God. This is supported by God's statement in verse 3:22. *"And the Lord God said, Behold, the man is become as one of us, to know good and evil: and now, lest he put forth his hand, and take also of the tree of life, and eat, and live for ever."* This verse tells us that Adam and Eve were already somewhat like God, in that they had some Godly characteristics. They were lacking only the ability to distinguish between good and evil. They were even immortal. Only after consuming the forbidden fruit was immortality taken from them. That is why they had been told if they ate of the fruit they would surely die. If they had not eaten of the fruit they would not have become mortal.

Since the forbidden fruit gave them only the ability to know good and evil and took from them only immortality, if we have any other Godly characteristics they must have already possessed them. The fact we have some of the characteristics of God is why He felt it was good to give us dominion over all of the other animals on the Earth. When God said man would be made in his likeness, He was saying we would be made to be like Him, not necessarily to look like Him.

God had told Adam not to eat of the fruit of a certain tree and warned him that if he did he would surely die. It was at the point of consuming the forbidden fruit that death entered the bodies of Adam and Eve. This death had nothing to do with the humans I believe were created before. It had only to do with Adam and those who would follow. The fruit of the Tree of Life would have served as an antidote for death. God could not allow a physical man who had the knowledge of evil to be also immortal. That is why he protected the Tree of Life from man by evicted the couple from the Garden of Eden. He had already gone through that in Heaven with Lucifer (Satan).

Since I believe the male and female created in Chapter 1 are not Adam and Eve, it bears the question of whether the first humans were immortal. No, I do not believe the beings of the chapter one creation were immortal. Neither do I believe the animals of chapter one were immortal. They both lived and died in a normal life cycle. I think immortality is one way God made Adam and Eve different from the first man. The fact Adam was different from the other humans is the reason God planted a special garden for him and placed him in it. Adam was being isolated from the 'lesser' humans. That could be another entire discussion. Since the dinosaurs are the primary focus of this work I will not spend too much time explaining that statement. I will admit I have not read a biblical passage to support it. Of course most traditionalists teach there was absolutely no death on the earth before Adam's sin. If non-traditionalists believe death began with Adam then the first humans would also have been immortal. Since they were not descendents of Adam they would not have been affected by his sin. All of them would have lived until the time of the flood. They may even have survived the flood. Those commercials with the cave man may be reality T.V.

We are made to resemble the image God had pre-planned for us, and to have His characteristics, or to be like him. That is how we were made in His image and likeness. Though we are not the descendants of the first humans, God still made us in His image and likeness when he formed Adam from the ground and Eve from Adam. The things that made Adam different was that God decided to withhold from Adam the knowledge of good and evil and give him immortality. Also, since God was simply forming a new man, He did make us to look like the first humans he created.

Support of this explanation of image and likeness can be found in the book of Philippians. Chapter two, verses 5 through 8 read, "*5Let this mind be in you, which was also in Christ Jesus: 6Who, being in the form of God, thought it not robbery to be equal with God: 7But made Himself of no reputation, and took upon him the form of a servant, and was made in the likeness of men: 8And being found in fashion (appearance) as a man, he humbled himself, and became obedient unto death, even the death of the cross.*" These verses tell us the form of Jesus before he became a man was different than His form as a man. He had to take on the form of man which means our form was not his original form. It wasn't until He took on that form and was made in the likeness of men that He was found in the appearance of a man. Originally He was in the same form as God. That tells us the two forms are different. Neither Genesis 1:26 nor 2:7 says God mad man in His form. Since the two forms are different, the teaching that we look like God is not supported by scripture. Scripture would indicate we do not look like God. Jesus had to be made to look like us.

The verses in Philippians along with Genesis 1:26 also take us back to what I see as one of the flaws in traditional teaching. Philippians 2:6 indicates that even before Jesus became man, He and God were two separate entities. In Genesis 1:26 God said, "*Let us...*" The word 'us' would also indicate more than one entity. In making that statement I do not mean to indicate I do not believe they are of the same spirit. I believe they are. I simply believe we are to view the Father, the Son, and the Holy Spirit from the purpose they serve in our lives. I believe the teaching of God the Father, God the Son, and God the Holy Spirit is in error. The traditional teaching of the Trinity may not be biblically accurate. That teaching is one of the things that were infused into the Christian religion by the Roman Empire through a council formed and run by the Emperor. While the discussion of that particular topic is not the point of this work, I only use it emphasize that some of our traditional religious teaching has human rather than biblical origins. With that in mind, as we discuss the biblical indicators of the dinosaurs being a part of God's creation, we need to not hold too strongly to traditional teaching.

The discussion of verse 1:26 was necessary to establish the foundation for what is to be discussed in more detail later. That is; the male and female of the species man, who were created in chapter one verse 27, were not Adam and Eve. That is a major issue when discussing the dinosaurs in the Bible. Just as the male and female of chapter one are not Adam and Eve, the animals created in chapter one are not the same animals formed in chapter two.

To begin the discussion of the differences in the chronologies of chapters one and two we must read the passage that begins with verse 31 of chapter 1 and continues through verse three of chapter two. It is easy to see the coherence of the verses. *"1:31 And God saw every thing that He had made, and, behold, it was very good. And the evening and the morning were the sixth day. 2:1 Thus the heavens and the earth were finished, and all the host of them. 2 And on the seventh day God ended His work which He had made; and He rested on the seventh day from all His work which He had made. 3 And God blessed the seventh day, and sanctified it: because that in it He had rested from all His work which God created and made."* It is obvious that, if read without the verse numbers, the first three verses of chapter two concludes chapter one. This is intended to be one continuous passage. The word 'thus' at the beginning of chapter two, verse one, shows that verse is connected to the previous passages. Verses two and three both begin with the word 'and' which shows they are also connected. The seventh day, the day of rest, was the conclusion of God's original act of creation as described in chapter one, not the beginning of something new as the chapter numbers would insinuate. A new discussion started with chapter two, verse four. It will become evident later why this distinct difference from traditional teaching is so important.

It may be very difficult to find a Christian pastor or priest who believes a perfect GOD would change his mind about his creation. Why would GOD change his mind if his creation was perfect to begin with? Verse 31 of chapter one states that God saw His creation was *"very good."* Maybe it should not be seen as a change, but rather as an addition or alteration to His creation. After all He did not speak anything new into existence. He took material He had already created and formed the new creatures. I do not claim to be able to explain the reasons GOD does what HE does. Isaiah 55:8 says, *"For my thoughts are not your thoughts, neither are your ways my ways, saith the Lord."* However, I do believe that the Bible tells us God decided to form new creatures in chapter two. The reason He made that decision may also be written. That reason will also be brought out in this study.

The Bible does show us in Genesis 6:6&7 that God does change His mind. *"And it repented the Lord that He had made man on the earth, and it grieved him at his heart. And the Lord said, I will destroy man whom I have created from the face of the earth; both man, and beast, and the creeping thing, and the fowls of the air; for it repenteth Me the I have made them."* In that particular case it was because of mans behavior. I simply contend that the passage in chapter six is not the first time God chose to alter His creation. It is not because His creation was imperfect. It may be because the creatures became imperfect. At any rate, I believe chapters one and two of Genesis are accounts of two different acts of creation and formation of the creatures that would inhabit the land on the Earth. There is no way to know what God's true reason was for forming the second group of beings.

The argument religious teachers will use against this is verse two of chapter two. *"And on the seventh day God ended his work which he had made; and he rested on the seventh day from all his work which he had made."* We are taught that nothing else was created or made after God rested. But that is not what that verse actually says. Nor is there a verse that teaches that. Yes He rested after His initial creation but did He stop working? More to the point, did He never do any more work? The verse simply says He rested. Don't we teach that He continues to perform miracles? Doesn't He continue to bless? Did the locus and flies of the plagues on Egypt gather from all over the world or did God make them for that purpose? Unless you can show me a verse in the Bible where God said He would not make anything new, the argument has no foundation.

Actually my belief does not totally contradict that argument. Since Adam and the animals of chapter two were formed from the ground, there wasn't actually anything new created. (In the strictest sense of the word) God simply took what He had already created (soil) and formed it into other beings. From a human perspective that act may be still seen as an act of creation. That is why I may still use the word creation to describe it. Even we (humans) can take things from the ground and form objects from it. We just don't have God's power to give the object life. God took non-living soil, shaped it, and breathed life into it to make it a living soul.

The exception to this would seem to be the plants that were created (Gen. 2:5) to be planted in the Garden of Eden. *And every plant of the field before it was in the earth, and every herb of the field before it grew...* These plants were created anew 'before' they were in the earth. The plants of chapter one were brought fourth (1:12) from the earth. *"And the earth brought forth grass, and herb yielding seed after his kind, and the tree yielding fruit, whose seed was in itself, after his kind; and God saw that it was good."* One group of plants being brought forth 'from' the earth and the other being made 'before' they were in the earth is a difference that shows these can not be the same plants. The statement of chapter 2:5 is not a restatement of chapter 1:12.

The greatest evidence for the statement that there were two different creations of creatures comes from studying and comparing the chronologies of the order of the creations in both chapters. The chronology of chapter one is established by the Word of God stating the day on which each set of creatures was created. Because it is clearly stated which creatures were created on which day, it is not possible to change the order of the chapter one creations. Also, the completion of each step is signified by the statement 'and God saw that it was good'. On the other hand the chronology of the second chapter is established by the Word of God stating the reasons God created each set of creatures when He did. Because the reasons are clearly stated why God created the creatures when he did, it is also not possible to change the order of the chapter two creations.

Most religious leaders that say chapter two is a re-statement of chapter one, more specifically day six of chapter one, will attempt to justify that common teaching by saying the acts of creation written in one of the two chapters may not be in chronological order. As I have already stated, the days stated on which God created the creatures (ch. 1), and the reasons He gave for creating the creatures when He did (ch. 2), clearly establishes both chronologies are correct and unchangeable. Therefore, that argument is invalid. The chronologies of the creations in chapters one and two do not match. Since neither can be changed, they must be statements of two different sets of events. The Bible is the truth and does not contradict itself.

Let us make a thorough comparison of the chronologies of the two chapters. First, chapter one is the only chapter that gives a detailed account of the creation and formation of light, the heavens, and the earth (vs. 1-10). This time was described as the first, second, and the beginning of the third day. Since only the living organisms that would inhabit the land were created new in chapter two, there was no need to recreate the heavens and earth. The new organisms of chapter two were placed on the already existing Earth. That is why there is no account in chapter two of this part of the creation. If chapter two is simply a re-statement of chapter one, that part of the creation would also have been re-stated. Many religious teachers discount this omission by saying chapter two is only a restatement of day six.

As we study, we will see that not only is the chronology of events in chapters one and two obviously different, but the methods of creation were also different between the two chapters. The traditional teaching about the methods of creation states that all creatures were spoken into existence except man. Man was formed by God's own hands. This explanation is pleasing to the ears because it allows man to establish himself as being special to God. While that claim is not necessary because God had already created man in his own image and likeness and given man dominion over the other animals, man's ego still needed to be stroked a little more to be satisfied. However, we will discuss why that teaching is not necessarily accurate. The difference is often overlooked because most people are taught about the creation before they ever read it for themselves. As they then read the passages, they will simply see what they have been taught. That is common among humans. This study will hopefully allow you to see what is actually written.

Of the living organisms, the plants were the first things created in both chapters. There are differences, however, in the circumstances surrounding the creations.

>ch. 1) vs. 11-13
>
>11And god said, Let the earth bring forth grass, the herb yielding seed, and the fruit tree yielding fruit after his kind, whose seed is in itself, upon the earth: and it was so. 12And the earth brought forth grass, and herb yielding seed after his kind, and the tree yielding fruit, whose seed was in itself, after his kind: and God saw that it was good. 13And the evening and the morning were the third day.

ch. 2)   vs. 4-6

4These are the generations of the heavens and of the earth when they were created, in the day that the Lord God made the earth and the heavens, 5And every plant of the field before it was in the earth, and every herb of the field before it grew: for the Lord God had not caused it to rain upon the earth, and there was not a man to till the ground. 6But there went up a mist from the earth, and watered the whole face of the ground.

Notice in chapter one the plants were spoken into existence on the third day. After God spoke, the plants simple grew out of the earth. The Earth brought forth the plants (1:12). There is no mention of any need of a source of moisture being necessary for the plants to grow. Simply because God spoke, they grew. Since the ground and waters had just been separated (vs. 9), and if current science was applicable at that time, there may have been enough moisture in the ground to allow for plant growth. Since I do not believe the scientific explanation of the evolution of the Earth, I believe the laws of physics that we observe today are the same as when God created the Heavens and the Earth. God did, after all, create the laws of physics when He created the universe. After God spoke, the earth brought forth the plant life. You must notice that man would not be created for another three days. This chapter one account is the only statement of plant creation traditionally taught by the majority of religious teachers.

Chapter two, in contrast, tells us there first had to be a source of water for the plants to grow. You must notice God created the plants of chapter two before they were in the earth and before they grew (2:5). I repeat; these plants were created before they were in the earth. They were not brought forth from the earth. He then caused a mist to rise from the earth for the reason He had not yet caused it to rain. The ground needed to be re-saturated. This could be an indication that enough time had passed since the intial creation for the excess ground water to have evaporated or seeped into the oceans, lakes, rivers or underground streams. How much time that would have taken I will not try to estimate. The underground streams could be from where He caused the mist to rise.

It is also stated that a man was needed to till the ground. We will see later God planted the plants created in chapter two (2:8) only after the man (Adam) who would till the ground was formed (2:5). They did not just come forth from the ground by God's word as did the plants of chapter one. After God planted them He then made the plants grow (2:9). Note that in chapter one the plants grew three days before man was created. These were planted after man was formed. While I have heard some teachers combine the two accounts, I have not heard anyone point out the difference.

At this point we must take a closer examination of verse four of chapter two. This is the pivotal verse for making the distinction between what I believe the Bible says and the traditional teaching. *"These are the generations of the heavens and of the earth when they were created, in the day that the Lord God made the earth and the heavens."* How we understand this verse will make a huge difference in looking beyond traditional teaching. I have already stated that I feel this verse should be the first verse of chapter two. The King James translation uses the word 'generations' in this verse where other translations use the word 'history'. That is a huge difference because 'generations' would indicate levels of history. Teaching only one act of creation does not allow for the use of 'generations' to be accurate. This is where the Bible translation used makes a difference. The King James Bible was translated from the original text with the expressed purpose of having an accurate translation. Most other modern translations were written with ease of understanding being the primary motive. That includes the New King James Translation. Because one creation is generally the only lesson taught, 'history' is an easier word to use for understanding the verse in that context. If one creation were taught using the word 'generations' it would leave a question of how it applies. Although I have never heard a question asked about that particular word, I am sure the educated teachers would have a programmed response. Most teachers don't like unanswerable questions. I believe the answer to the question is that chapter two describes the second generation of God's creation.

The Hebrew word 'toledoth' is the word translated 'generations' in Genesis 2:4. It is derived from the Hebrew verb that means "to bear children." The same word is used when referring to the lineages of Adam (5:1), Noah (6:9), the sons of Noah (10:1), Terah (11:27), Ishmael (25:12), Isaac (25:19), Esau (36:1), and Jacob (37:2). In each case only the particular offspring was named that was important in the history of the earth, the Israelites, and mankind. Any other children mentioned were referred to simply as sons and daughters. This is most evident in the case of Adam. We know Adam and Eve first had Cain and Able then Seth (4:1, 2, & 25). However, when the 'generations' of Adam were named (5:1), Seth was the first named (5:3) although Cain and Able were the first two sons and Cain was still living in the land of Nod. "5:1 *This is the book of the generations of Adam. In the day that God created man, in the likeness of God made He him. 2Male and female created he them; and blessed them, and called their name Adam, in the day when they were created. 3And Adam lived an hundred and thirty years, and begat a son in his own likeness, after his image; and called his name Seth.*" This shows that the lineage of Seth was the one that bore the offspring that was important to the developing history of man on the Earth as recorded by Moses. Seth was named as the first in the 'generations' (toledoth) of Adam even with the fact we know Cain was the first born of Adam. By the same token the plants and creatures created and formed in chapter two were the 'generations' of the Earth even though there were creatures created before. The living organisms of chapter two are the ones that ultimately were the organisms that developed throughout the history of the Earth.

Just as Seth was the son of Adam who was important to the future human race, the creations of chapter two would be the living organisms that would bear the offspring that were important to the future of the Earth. They would be the ones that would be saved on the Ark. That is why they were called the 'generations' of the heavens and the earth. Just as Cain and Able were not mentioned in the 'generations' of Adam, the man and animals of chapter one were not mentioned in the 'generations' of the Earth. You must remember that when the Word was given to Moses to record, the events of Genesis were already history. The flood that destroyed all of the living creatures on the Earth was a part of that history. Moses recorded everything that was given to him by the Spirit. In the process, distinctions were made between those things that were important and unimportant. The word 'toledoth', translated 'generations', is one of the words used to make that distinction. That sets the creatures that were created in chapter two apart from those of chapter one. Not only are the creations of chapters one and two different, the organisms of the creations of chapter two were the 'generations' that would ultimately remain after the flood to re-populate the earth. At the time Moses recorded the Word they were the animals that had been saved on the ark and were alive on the Earth.

The interpretation of the phrase "when they were created"

(2:4) is also very important. The key is which tense of the word 'were' is read into the verse. The common explanation uses the present perfect tense to say it means 'at the time they were created.' I believe a thorough study will show that the past perfect tense is more accurate and that the verse means 'when they had already been created.' That is the reason God was able to go straight from the creation of the plants to the creation of man in chapter two. In Chapter one the creation of the sun, moon, and stars came after the creation of the plants. Once again if current science was applicable, and I believe it was, the plants would need the sunlight for growth. That would be why, in chapter one, the sun and others were the next in the order of the creation. Since the sun had already been created before chapter two, all the new plants needed were a source of water and someone to till the ground. That would be the mist from the earth and Adam. Only after Adam was formed did God plant the plants in the Garden of Eden. Once again, "when they were created" should be interpreted as 'the heavens and the earth were *already* created.'

The fourth creation day is not restated in chapter two.

> ch. 1) vs. 14-19
>
> 14And God said, Let there be lights in the firmament of the heaven to divide the day from the night; and let them be for signs, and for seasons, and for days, and years: 15And let them be for lights in the firmament of the heaven to give light upon the earth; and it was so: 16And God made two great lights; the greater light to rule the day, and the lesser light to rule the night: He made the stars also. 17And God set them in the firmament of the heaven to give light upon the earth, 18And to rule over the day and

over the night, and to divide the light from the darkness: and God saw that it was good. 19And the evening and the morning were the fourth day.

This is the only account of the creation of the sun, moon, and stars. There is no mention of their creation in chapter two. As I already stated, I believe the only things God recreated or formed in chapter two were the living organisms that would inhabit the land on the Earth. The other components needed for life, sun and water, had been created before. It is important that you notice this is the next chronological event in chapter one after the creation of the plants. The timing of this part of creation was established as the fourth day. Just as plants need sunlight today there was a need for the sun and others to be created for the plants of chapter one to remain alive. (Today's physics of Biology was created by God in the beginning.) They were also created for man to be able to measure time. In chapter two the next chronological event was the creation of man. The reason was given that there was not a man to till the ground. As I have already indicated, the chronology of events is critical in showing that chapter two is not a restatement of chapter one. The chronology of chapter one was stated in terms of days. The chronology of chapter two was established by reason. The plants, of chapter one, were created on the third day. The sun, moon, and stars were created on the fourth day.

After the fourth day creations of the sun, moon, and stars God created the sea creatures on the fifth day. If you take the celestial objects temporarily out of the order, the sea creatures were the living organisms created immediately after the plants in chapter one. Man was created immediately after the plants in chapter two.

ch. 1) vs. 20-23

20And God said, Let the waters bring forth abundantly the moving creature that hath life, and fowl that may fly above the earth in the open firmament of heaven. 21And God created great whales, and every living creature that moveth, which the waters brought forth abundantly, after their kind, and every winged fowl after his kind: and God saw that it was good. 22And God blessed them, saying, Be fruitful, and multiply, and fill the waters in the seas, and let fowl multiply in the earth. 23And the evening and the morning were the fifth day.

ch. 2) vs. 7

And the Lord God formed man of the dust of the ground, and breathed into his nostrils the breath of life; and man became a living soul.

Two days after God created the plants in chapter one He created the sea creatures and the birds. This passage is the only mention of the sea creatures being created. They, also, were not recreated in chapter two. These creatures would not inhabit the land. Since these creatures lived in the water, they would not be destroyed by the flood. While there have been fossils of now extinct sea creatures found, I have not seen any that were notably larger than modern whales. I have not seen any that would specifically or exclusively be put into the category of the dinosaur. Because the aquatic animals were not recreated there are no great differences that scientists have been able to use to feed the evolution myth. Even with the Cambrian Explosion (which will be discussed later) there are no significant new aquatic species found. Evolutionary scientists actually have had to try to connect aquatic animals to land animals. They created the story that fish crawled out of the water and started to walk.

The birds (winged fowl in vs. 1:21) would, however, inhabit the land (vs. 1:22) and were recreated in chapter two. Although they were created initially with the sea creatures they were to live on the land. Much to the scientist's dismay even at the point of creation the two sets of animals that were created together were distinctly different. Science has tried to connect them through evolution. There was no evolution from the fish to the birds. Because of the differences the birds were not able to live in the water. The fowls, of chapter one, were also not able to stay in flight for the duration of the flood and were therefore destroyed. That is why the fowls were re-created in chapter two. We will see later the fowls of chapter two were placed on the Ark by God and were saved. That is also why the fowls of chapter two were within the generations of the Earth.

A very important point to re-emphasize here is that the birds of the chapter one group were created along with the sea creatures and they were both brought forth from the water. I point that out because this is another very distinct difference from chapter two. As we will see the birds were created with the land animals in chapter two. The land animals had not been created at this time in chapter one. They will not be created until the morning of the next day. It is also important to notice that in chapter one the birds were created a full day before man. In chapter two they were created after Adam was formed. For those that will say chapter two is only a detailed account of day six, this, along with the day three plants, presents a problem.

Some traditionalists who use other translations will argue the birds did not come from the water. Without getting too much into that argument they can not deny these fowls were created on the same day as the fish and before man. The chapter two fowls were created with the land animals and after Adam. Those two points still make it undeniable these fowls are not the same fowls of chapter two.

The order of creation in chapter one was done at God's discretion. In chapter two it was by His reason. Man was created after the plants in chapter two by reason that "there was not a man to till the ground" (vs.2:5). By the same reason those plants were not planted until the ground tiller was formed. Notice also that no other creatures, excluding the sea creatures which were created in chapter one, were created before man in chapter two. That includes the birds. Another difference that must be noted is that woman was not created with man in chapter two. Adam was created alone. At a later point God gave a reason for creating Eve.

One thing the religious leaders are proud to point out are the facts that, in chapter two, man was formed by God and that by God's own breath did man become a living soul. They use these to show man was special to God; once again feeding their ego. The fact that God brought the animals to Adam to be named should be enough to accomplish that. I think the two facts are more important for showing a difference between the creations of chapters one and two. This will be made more evident as we continue to study the order of the creations.

After creating the fish and fowls in chapter one, God created the animals that would inhabit the land.

> ch. 1)  vs. 24-25
> 24And God said, Let the earth bring forth the living creature after his kind, cattle, and creeping thing, and beast of the earth after his kind: and it was so. 25And God made the beast of the earth after his kind, and cattle after their kind, and every thing that

creepeth upon the earth after his kind: and God saw that it was good.

Here is where, in chapter one, God created the animals that would live on the land. These creatures were brought forth from the earth by God speaking. The end of verse 24 says *"and it was so"*. This is consistent with all of the creation of chapter one creatures. It is also consistent with traditional teaching. It is, however, different from the creations of the land animals in chapter two, as we will see later. Notice again that man had not been created at this point. Even though these animals were created in the same day as man, you can be sure, by the statement, *"and God saw that it was good"*, this step in the creation process was completed first. That statement was made at the end of each step of creation signifying the completion of each particular step. Therefore it is easy to see this step in creation (the land animals {dinosaurs}) was complete before the creation act of the following verse (man). The land animals of chapter one were the next creatures created after the sea animals and fowls and before the species man.

I did not pair any verses from chapter two with this passage because in chapter two, after creating man, God took a break from creating and made a home for the man; the Garden of Eden. That is where God planted the plants He created before they were in the Earth. Why did God find a need to make a special place for this man if he was the first man on the Earth? All of the earth would have been his home. All of the Earth would have been a paradise. There must have been some other reason. I will address this question in more detail later.

It is my contention that the animals whose creation was described in chapter one, verses 24-25, are the animals we now call dinosaurs. You must remember the word dinosaur will not be found in the Bible. That word was first used in the mid 1800's to describe the animals that must have belonged to the large bones that were being discovered. Bones were being discovered that did not match any species known to man at that time. They definitely did not match any species man had seen alive within the period of recorded history. Because the archeologists thought the bones may have been those of big lizards, dinosaur is the name they gave to these mysterious creatures. Big lizard is the definition of the word dinosaur. I contend that these 'dinosaur' bones belong to the animals that were created in chapter one. These animals are different from the animals which, chronologically, have yet to be created in chapter two.

ch. 1) vs. 26-28

26And God said, Let us make man in our image, after our likeness: and let them have dominion over the fish of the sea, and over the cattle, and over all the earth, and over every creeping thing that creepeth upon the earth. 27So God created man in his own image, in the image of God created He him, male and female created He them. 28And God blessed them, and God said unto them, Be fruitful, and multiply, and replenish the earth, and subdue it; and have dominion over the fish of the sea, and over the fowl of the air, and over every living thing that moveth upon the earth.

ch. 2) vs. 18-20a

18And the Lord God said, It is not good that the man should be alone; I will make him an help meet for him. 19And out of the ground the Lord God formed every beast of the field, and every fowl of the air; and brought them unto Adam to see what he would call them: and whatsoever Adam called every living creature, that was the name thereof. 20aAnd Adam gave names to all cattle, and to the fowl of the air, and to every beast of the field;

I repeat myself when I say in chapter one the animals had already been created before the account of the creation of man. The words that are written establish that fact. You must also notice that in chapter one male and female where created at the same time (1:27). This is another important difference between the chapters. The species was called man. Just as with any other species there was a male and female. There is no mention of the female being made from the male. That would be why the name 'woman' was not use in chapter one to describe the female. Also, God gave **them** (1:28) dominion over all living things. The species man (male and female), who was created **last**, would have dominion over the other species that were created before. It seems God gave the same charge only to Adam in chapter two. The animals were brought before only Adam to be named. Eve had not been formed at that point.

In Chapter two, by reason that it was not good for Adam to be alone, the land animals were the next creatures created by God after Adam. Once again I point out that Adam was formed **first**. The animals were formed to be helpers to Adam. The woman, Eve, had not been formed at this point. Another reason will be given for her formation. These points are distinctly different from chapter one. God had already found His creation of the animals of chapter one to be "good" before chapter one man was created. Therefore, that man would not have been alone in the way Adam was. The primary point: in chapter one first the animals then man; in chapter two first the man then the animals.

The reason Adam was alone was because God set him in the

Garden of Eden, away from the other people. Yes, I know that is not written. But, if this had been the first creation all of the Earth would have been like a beautiful garden. A special garden would not have been necessary. At any rate, the reason stated in Chapter two, verse 18 clearly establishes the order of the creations of man and animals. First the reason was given. Adam was alone and it was not good. Next the solution was given. A helper would be made for him. "19*And out of the ground the Lord God formed every beast of the field...*" The order is different from chapter one. Both orders are clearly established and are unchangeable. The creation of Adam and the animals in chapter two is not a re-statement of chapter one or day six. Adam was initially alone because he was place in an isolated garden. The man in chapter one would not have been alone. He and the female were created together and after the animals.

There are two other important points to be noticed here. The first is that the fowl of the air were created with the land animals in chapter two (2:19). "*...formed every beast of the field, and every fowl of the air...*" They were created with the sea animals in chapter one (1:20)....*waters bring forth abundantly the moving creatures creature that hath life, and fowl that may fly above the earth...*" One can not say it is a matter of interpretation because the fowls and the land animals were created on different days in chapter one. The fowls were created on day five and the land animals on day six. They were created a full day apart. This difference helps to re-emphasize the importance of recognizing that the statements of days clearly establishes the order of creation in chapter one while the statements of reason does the same in chapter two.

The second point is that God used different methods of creation in the two chapters. In chapter one the fowls came forth from the water and the land animals came forth from the ground after God spoke to make it so. In chapter two they were both formed by God from the ground. I put emphasis on the word formed. In chapter one, they were spoken into existence. That is the method of creation that is generally taught traditionally for all living organisms except man. In chapter two the land animals and fowls were formed by God just as man had been. Re-read verses 2:7 and 2:19. This is the difference in the methods of creation between the two chapters that most people overlook. We tend to read into the text what we have been previously taught. This very important difference clearly indicates the two creature creations are distinctly different. The two sets of land animals are distinctly different. The dinosaurs were spoken into existence and brought fourth (not formed) from the ground. Modern animals were formed from the ground. As I will discuss in detail later, the creatures that were formed are the ones that were saved on the Ark and that we see today.

Let us focus for a minute primarily on the fowls. There is a huge difference between God speaking and the fowls being brought forth from the water (1:20-21) and God actually forming the fowls from the land (2:19). There is no way to say one is a re-statement of the other. The fowls of chapter one and the fowls of chapter two are different. The Pterodactyls and other flying dinosaurs were brought forth from the water. They were definitely created with the fish. The Eagle, Robin, and other flying creatures of today were formed from the ground and with the land animals. The formed fowls were within the generation that would be saved.

Most teachers, that I have heard, try to give the impression that only man was formed by God. Some will actually make that statement out right, coupled with the statement that all other creatures were spoken into existence. That is how they try to set man apart from the rest of God's creatures. It doesn't seem to be enough that God gave man dominion over them all in chapter one. It is apparent the same was true in chapter two seeing that He brought all of the animals to Adam to be named. It was also evident after the flood when God to Noah and his family all of the animals would fear them. As I stated before, this erroneous teaching seems to be a product of man's ego rather than Biblical study. At any rate, the animals of chapter two were formed by God (vs. 2:19) just as Adam had been (vs.2:7).

One thing I think is important to notice is the man in chapter one was spoken into existence as a living soul. Adam was formed from the ground and received the breath of life from God to become a living soul. The animals that were formed would also have needed the breath of life from God to become alive. It is not that God could not have made them already alive, but that He chose to make them different than He did the first group of animals. The true importance of this point will be made evident in the discussion of how the dinosaurs died.

Man (male and female) was the last creature created in chapter one. All other creatures had been created before man. After the creation of man in chapter one God's acts of the original creation were concluded.

> ch. 2) vs. 1-3
> 1Thus the heavens and the earth were finished; and all the host of them. 2And on the seventh day God ended His work which He had made; and He rested on the seventh day from all His work which He had made. 3And God blessed the seventh day, and sanctified it: because that in it He had rested from all His work which God created and made.

These are the verses that tell us God had finished what he originally "created and made." That is precisely why I think these verses should have been the end of chapter one. Even these verses re-enforce the chronology of chapter one as being in terms of days. This was the seventh day. The days were actual measures of time based on the sun, moon, and stars, not figurative measures. Some scientists say they were just theological measures. They were distinguished by the evening and the morning. Certain named acts of creation were completed on certain named days. The completion of each act was signified by the statement, "and God saw that it was good." These statements should make it obvious the chronological order of the individual creations in chapter one can not be changed. Day seven was the end of the original acts of creation.

The statement "*and God was that it was good*" is a very significant statement. That statement definitely establishes an ending to each phase or step in the creation process (Genesis 1:4, 10, 12, 18, 21, 25, & 31). A believer should never say the earth and life developed through a gradual evolutionary process. To say so is the say you do not believe what the Bible says. How can a person, scientist or otherwise, say he is a Christian, say the Bible is the Word of God, read the statements mentioned, then turn around and say he believed evolution happened?

Man was not the last creature formed in chapter two. There was a reason given by God why He formed Adam when He did (to till the ground). There was also a reason given by God why he continued with the acts of creature formation after Adam (he was alone). Even after the land animals were formed Adam was no longer alone but was still lonely. Because of that, the reason was given by God why He would create Adams female mate, the woman Eve (2:20b).

ch.2)   vs. 20b-25

20bbut for Adam there was not found an help meet for him. 21And the Lord God caused a deep sleep to fall upon Adam, and he slept: and He took one of his ribs, and closed up the flesh instead thereof; 22And the rib, which the Lord God had taken from man, made He a woman, and brought here unto the man. 23And Adam said, This is now bone of my bones, and flesh of my flesh: she shall be called Woman, because she was taken out of Man. 24Therefore shall a man leave his father and his mother, and shall cleave unto his wife; and they shall be one flesh. 25And they were both naked, the man and his wife, and were not ashamed.

By reason that there was not found a helper among the animals that was comparable to Adam, God made woman (Eve). Eve, alone, was the last creature formed in chapter two. Adam had been formed alone and prior to the other animals. The reasons given by God establishes the unchangeable order in which the creatures were formed in chapter two; first Adam, then the land animals, then Eve. In chapter one the male and female had been created together. Both were created after the animals. These are unmistakable and unchangeable differences between the two chapters.

Some traditionalists will say the formation of the animals is verse 19 is not necessarily because of Adam being alone. They say chapter one is in chronological order but chapter two is not. The teaching is that verse 2:19 is just a reminder that God had created the animals. They can not give a reason why this account would be stuck between the formation of Adam and Eve. Does it make sense that God would have Moses record verse in such a confusing manner?

These events, in fact, are recorded in chronological order. The key word that verifies this is the word 'but' in verse 20. The conjunction connects verses 19 and 20 back to the condition of Adam's loneliness in verse 18. When verse 20 ends with "*but for Adam there was not found an help meet for him*", that supports the reason for the formation of the animals at that time. The reason was that Adam was alone and that was not good. The animals were formed to relieve the condition of him being alone. 'But' the condition was not totally relieved because the animals were not comparable to Adam. The use of the word 'but' confirms the events of chapter two are in chronological order.

Again, the reasons given for the different acts of creation in chapter two establishes the chronology of the formations. Man was formed to till the ground. The animals were formed because Adam was alone. Eve was formed because there was still not anyone comparable to Adam. This order is defined by reasons given by God. This order was different from the order defined by the days in chapter one. The animals were created at the beginning of the sixth day. The fact "*God saw that it was good*" (1:25) clearly establishes the fact that they were completed before God said, "*Let us make man...*" (1:25). The male and female of the species of man were created together and were the last creatures created.

I know I have repeated myself several times but I felt it was necessary to emphasize what is probably the most crucial point when discussing the Bible and the dinosaurs. When you compare the order of events, as I have shown above, it should be obvious the two chapters are describing two different accounts. The days established the chronology of chapter one. The reasons established the chronology of chapter two. Neither of them can be changed. To deny this is to say one of the two chapters is not accurate. I believe the Bible is not only the truth, but is also accurate.

All of the previous discussion provides the answer for the

primary question. We know animals once existed that were in some cases larger and very different than the animals of today. We have found the bones. We know the history of Earth as told in the Bible starts "In the beginning." To be complete, these two bits of information must come together. That brings us back to the question 'Where are these animals we have named dinosaurs mentioned in the Bible'? I feel I have clearly shown that God created two distinctly different groups of creatures that would inhabit the Earth. God (Ch. 1) spoke one group into existence. God (Ch. 2) formed the other group from the Earth. It is my belief, and I think careful study of the scriptures supports my belief, that the creatures created in chapter one of Genesis are the animals we have come to call Dinosaurs and the humans we call pre-historic (Neanderthal & Cro-Magnon). The creatures that were formed in chapter two are the animals and humans that were saved on the ark and exist today and that we would call modern.

The dinosaurs are the animals that were brought forth from the Earth. Genesis 1:24-25. *"24 And God said, let the earth bring forth the living creature after his kind, cattle, and creeping thing, and beast of the earth after his kind;* **and it was so.** *25 And God made the beast of the earth after his kind, and cattle, after their kind, and every thing that creepeth upon the earth after his kind; and God saw that it was good."*

# The Co-Existence of Man and Dinosaur

Before new information which is so different from what we have been taught will be believed and accepted, the old information must be shown to be erroneous. An important part of the evolutionary teaching is that dinosaurs and humans did not co-exist. We are taught there were millions of years between the two. For anyone who believes in the Bible it should be easy to see this information is wrong. However, since most traditional religious teachers do not address the subject the obvious is not so obvious.

Another component of the discussion is what happened to the dinosaur if they did live at the same time as man. Most traditionalists hold to the idea that they died after leaving the ark. They teach that all animals that ever existed were taken aboard the ark. The dinosaurs were not able to adapt to the environmental changes and died off. I do not believe the dinosaurs were taken aboard the ark at all. As we continue to study God's word I think you will see the dinosaur died in the flood with all of the other living creatures.

The animals in chapter one (dinosaurs) were created before man just as scientists have said. The Bible supports that statement. Where scientists are wrong is the time frame. Obviously the Bible does not describe the millions of years scientists say have passed. The dinosaur and man were created within the same 24 hour period. The entire sum of years described in the bible can only be numbered in the thousands. I will allow the biblical scholars to put an actual number on those thousands. At any rate, the millions-of-years theories are not accurate. In order to give the dinosaurs and prehistoric man their own times, then give time to modern animals and man, scientists first theorized the time to be millions of years. That was necessary to allow for the theory of evolution to be believable. They then devised a system of dating objects (radiometric dating) that would support, or in their words prove, their theory. Even when using their system scientists use the words estimate or approximate when they mention their results. I will show that any logical thinking Christian or non-Christian who examines the scientist's system objectively will know the system could not be accurate.

Scientists also say dinosaurs and pre-historic man did not co-exist. The Bible shows them to be wrong on that count also. In both accounts of GOD creating man and animals He gave man dominion over the animals. Therefore, man and animal have always co-existed. Only a non-Christian/non-Jewish person could say they did not co-exist. The irony is the same scientists that will teach evolution will sit next to you in church. But, can a person truly be Jewish or Christian and not believe what is written in the Bible. If you are a believer in the Word of God there is no doubt that the animals and humans created by God co-existed. The only question, then, left to be answered is did the animals and men of the first creation co-exist with those of the second?

There is no way to know how much time passed between the

two chapters. It was definitely not millions of years. It was long enough for natural processes to allow the excess ground water to seep into lakes, oceans, rivers, or gather in underground streams. That is why there was a need for a source of water for the new plants. Despite the amount of time, I believe the two sets of creatures co-existed from the point of the second creation until the great flood.

If the two groups of chapters one and two did not co-exist there would have been some biblical account of the first group being destroyed before the formation of the beings in chapter two. Once again, I believe the Bible gives us all of the information we need to explain the things we observe. The traditionalist's 'gap' theory does not give us the information. Because we have observed the remains of the dinosaur and pre-historic man, we know they existed. These creatures do not still exist, yet the Bible makes no statement of global destruction before the great flood. Therefore, the absence of a statement of destruction would indicate the first creation beings were still on the earth at the time of the second. Not only do I believe that to be the case, their co-existence answers several other questions that will be addressed later. Also, as I stated earlier, I believe the people of the first creation are the ones Adam was being isolated from when God placed him in the Garden of Eden.

In chapter two, verse eight God planted the garden at Eden and placed Adam in it. That is the reason God made the statement, "It is not good that man should be alone" (2:18). Most will say the statement shows that Adam was the only creature made at that time. If he had been the man of chapter one he would not have been the only creature at the time of his creation. All of the other animals were created before him. Also he would have already had a mate. The male and female were created together in chapter one. Therefore, he would not have been alone.

I believe Adam was alone because God had isolated him from the remainder of Earth's beings. All other beings had been spoken into existence. Adam was the only one, at this point, that had been formed from the ground and had received the "breathe of life" directly from God. The creatures of chapter one, including the species man, had not been created the same and therefore was not 'comparable' to him. He (Adam) was special. God was keeping the new man separate from the others. That is why God also formed out of the ground the animals of chapter two when HE was creating a helper "comparable" to Adam. The beings that were spoken into existence were not comparable to the formed being. I re-state also, the animals of chapter two were formed after Adam and before Eve. (The animals in chapter one were created before both the male and female of the species man.) Eve was then formed from Adam because these animals were still not comparable in form (shape and abilities). Adam was initially alone because of location not order of creation.

This idea would be rejected by most because, once again, it raises the question why God would choose to change His creation. Even if the first creatures were spoken into existence, the fact God did the speaking would make them perfect at the time of their creation. People will say the method of creation, speaking or forming, would not make a difference since God did them both. I agree with that statement. Why, then, would God feel the need to separate the two groups? That is a question I could only speculate about. Maybe the first creatures had in some way become imperfect over time just as we have. I repeat myself again by saying I will not actually try to explain God's thoughts or the unwritten reasons for His actions. The Bible tells us we should not. Yet, I believe the Bible teaches that there were two different creations of earth's creatures. God chose to separate Adam from the group of the first creation. That is why God planted the

Garden of Eden and placed Adam in it. If chapter two was a continuation, or restatement, of everything that had been created new, there would not have been a reason to plant a separate garden for Adam. Everything would have still been plush and beautiful.

The co-existence of the creatures of the two creations answers two other often asked questions. First; who were the people Cain was afraid would harm him (4:14)? Second; from where did Cain's wife come (4:17)? The common argument to answer both questions is that there is no way to know how much time had passed and that the events are not necessarily in chronological order. Teachers who use that argument will say that the offspring of Adam and Eve's other children had populated the earth by that time and Cain married one of his distant relatives. I even read one explanation that said he married either his sister or his niece. I disagree with those explanations.

Cain's punishment was given by God immediately after his crime (4:8-15). The word 'and' at the beginning of verse nine (and various other verses) clearly connects the verses and indicates no long period of time had passed. "8*And Cain talked with Abel his brother; and it came to pass, when they were in the field, that Cain rose up against Abel his brother, and slew him.* 9**And** *the Lord said unto Cain, where is Abel they brother? And he said, I know not; am I my brother's keeper?* 10*And He said, What hast thou done? The voice of thy brother's blood crieth unto me from the ground.* 11*And now art thou cursed from the earth, which hath opened her mouth to receive thy brother's blood from thy hand;* 12*When thou tillest the ground it shall not henceforth yield unto thee her strength; a fugitive and a vagabond shalt thou be in the earth.* 13*And Cain said unto the Lord, My punishment is greater than I can bear.* 14*Behold, thou hast driven me out this day from the face of the earth; and from thy face shall I be hid; and I shall be a fugitive and a vagabond in the earth; and it shall come to pass that every one that findeth me shall slay me.* 15*And* *the Lord said unto him, Therefore whosoever slayeth Cain, vengeance shall be taken on him sevenfold. And the Lord set a mark upon Cain, lest any finding him should kill him."* God addressed Cain immediately after the crime was committed. Furthermore, the conversation between God and Cain was a continuous conversation that led to God giving Cain his punishment of exile. It is obvious from reading the fourth chapter of Genesis that Adam and Eve had not had any other children at the time of Cain's crime and exile. Yet, he was afraid of someone at the very time his punishment was given. The only reasonable explanation is that there were other people already on the earth he was already aware of. *"…and it shall come to pass, that every one that findeth me shall slay me"* (4:14). God's response to Cain also indicates the existence of other people. *"…And the Lord set a mark upon Cain, lest any finding him should kill him"* (4:15).

Adam, Eve, and family were no longer isolated from the rest of the world. After Adam and Eve ate the forbidden fruit their isolation in the Garden of Eden ended. *"3:23 Therefore the Lord God sent him forth from the Garden of Eden, to till the ground from whence he was taken. 24 So he drove out the man; and he placed at the east of the Garden of Eden cherubims, and a flaming sword which turned every way, to keep the way of the tree of life."* Their children (which included Cain) would be born in the world and be aware of its inhabitants. Although they were no longer isolated, I believe God was still protecting them in some way noticeable to them. Now that Cain was being exiled he knew he would lose that protection. That is why he was afraid. As God's goodness never changes, He still provided protection for Cain, by means of a mark, even in his punishment.

After he was assured by God he would not be harmed, Cain went out and found a wife. *"And Cain went out from the presence of the Lord, and dwelt in the land of Nod, on the east of Eden. And Cain knew his wife;…"* (4:16-17a). There is nothing in these verses that would indicate enough time had passed for any of Adam and Eve's other children to have grown to maturity and multiplied. That is simply the easiest explanation for traditionalists to continue with the one creation teachings. The use of the word 'and' once again connects the verses in question. God put a mark on Cain for protection **and** Cain immediately went out **and** Cain knew his wife. It is difficult to estimate how long it was from his exile to his taking a wife. Of course other things would have been going on during this period of time, but I do not believe there is any indication Adam and Eve's other children were in any way involved. In fact, I believe all of these things took place before Adam and Eve had any other children. If Cain's siblings had been involved the time frame would have been significant. God's word would have made the time frame clear just as He did when Adam's age was given at the mention of Seth's birth.

I have seen or been told of two objections to this idea. One objection is stated that God would not have allowed Cain to mate with a lower species. Of course this statement would have been made by someone who could first accept the two different groups of humans. The argument is that God clearly stated that each species would reproduce only after their "own kind." The second objection is an attempt to use this as proof of evolution of man, which I say didn't happen. Of course both objections carry no weight.

Concerning the first objection: Despite the fact the two groups of humans were brought into existence by different methods (spoken and formed) they were of the same species; man. The humans in who was the 'breath of life' had a spiritual difference from the first group. There was no physical difference. Both had been made in the image of God. (Gen. 1:27 & 5:1) Even with the spiritual advantage the behavior of both groups was still influenced by Satan. Satan (Lucifer) had been evited from heaven prior to the formation of Adam. His influence on the first beings is probably why God felt the need to re-create man and isolate him. That influence is why Adam and Eve ate of the fruit. That is also why Cain had just murdered Able. Although from different groups the species man was the same physically and behaviorally. That, in fact, is why Cain was afraid. He knew the other people were capable of behaving just as he had.

The second objection is more evidence that even some believers can not totally set aside ideas of evolution. They refuse to accept the possibility of two groups of humans without saying evolution is somehow involved. They think the mating of Cain, and future children of Adam and Eve, to members of the first group of humans somehow proves there was evolution of the human species. The mixing of the two groups would have produced a third group that was somehow physically better (or worse). In an effort to support their idea they first refer to the first group as sub-human. Of course the sub-human description is a direct result of the years of secular education where pre-historic man is described and portrayed as such. There is nothing in the Bible that would indicate the first group of the man species is any different physically than the second group. The secular description is aided by artist drawings. As a result, our evolutionary education influences us to simply read sub-human into the first group. The first group, compared to the second, was lacking only the "breath of life." The two groups were physically identical. The mating between the two groups is no more related to evolution than the mating of people of different races.

The Bible tells us Seth was the next child born to Adam and Eve. However, all of the events involving Cain happened before Seth was born. Seth wasn't born until Adam was 130 years old. Chapter four, verse 25 clearly indicates the situation with Cain happened before Seth. *"And Adam knew his wife again, and she bare a son, and called his name Seth, 'For God, said she, hath appointed me another seed instead of Abel, whom Cain slew.'"* Chapter five, verse four says Adam had other sons and daughters after Seth. *"And the days of Adam **after** he had begotten Seth were eight hundred years; and he begat sons and daughters".* Since Cain was exiled immediately after he slew Able, his younger siblings would not have come into play. The people Cain was afraid of, and from whom he found his wife, had to be on the Earth before he committed the crime and was exiled. I don't believe he waited 130 years before he found a wife. He was already aware of them and afraid of them when the punishment of his exile was given. They had to be from the group of the first creation. Cain was afraid of the other people and found his wife before Seth (and the other sons and daughters) was born (Gen. 4:16-17).

Many traditionalists and non-traditionalists alike will rationalize that Cain married either one of his sisters or a niece. They point out that there was a hundred or more years from Cain's exile until the Birth of Seth. They say Adam could have had many other children during that period and the population from Adam and Eve's descendants could have been in the thousands by that time. Of course all of those thousands would have to have been all girls since Seth was the next boy born to the couple. In that case you are saying Adam was having intercourse with his daughters. None of this is true. Besides, the Bible says Adam had other sons and daughters after Seth (Genesis 5:4). The people were already on the Earth. They are the people Cain was both afraid of and from whom he found his wife.

Eventually Seth would have had relation with one of his siblings. That is how the line to Noah would remain unaltered. The first humans had not received the breath of life. That would have produced a spiritual alteration, not physical, of Cain's line. Any of the other siblings who mated with the other group would have also had an altered line. That is why Seth was the generation of Adam that would lead to Noah and beyond.

Even with these questions answered, other very important questions must be asked and answered. Why do the animals of group one not still exist? When and how were they destroyed? These are questions that traditionalist all answer in pretty much the same way. They all say they became extinct after the flood. I don't believe that to be the case.

The only event in the Bible in which GOD destroyed all life on the land was the great flood. God's reason for destroying all flesh was given in chapter 6, verse 13, *"And God said unto Noah, 'The end of all flesh is come before Me, for the earth is filled with violence through them; and behold, I will destroy them with the earth.'"* This gives some possible credibility to scientists' descriptions of possible behaviors of the dinosaurs. Of course there is no true scientific evidence to support the idea, only speculation. Dinosaurs (and man) may have demonstrated violence toward each other without cause. That did not please God and was the reason for the flood. In contrast, the animals that remain today only attack when necessary for feeding or to protect its own. Even in a conflict over territory, when one animal is determined the victor, the conflict ends. The evidence of this is seen in many animal behavior films that document this behavior. Animals today do not commit acts of violence without cause (except humans). Exceptions to this would be cases in of an animal's illness or human influence. Since God's stated reason for bringing the flood was to destroy the violence from the earth, this difference would explain why GOD chose the animals we know today to be saved on the ark and the animals of the first creation (dinosaurs) to be destroyed.

The violence described in verse 6:13 could be a possible explanation of why God formed Adam and placed him in the garden. The degradation of the chapter one beings may have begun much earlier. The details of their lives would not be written because they are not of the generation that would be important in the development of the earth. If they had begun to demonstrate violence that could have been the reason God decided to form new creatures. It also would be a good reason for Adam to be isolated from them. This may also be an explanation of why Cain feared for his life. He was aware of them and their violent behavior. I must say this one paragraph is pure speculation and should be taken as such. But it makes sense.

The two objections to this idea from the traditionalists would be they teach there was no death before Adam's sin and there was no sin at all before Adam's sin. It is easy for them to say there was no death before Adam because they do not believe anything lived before him. I believe there was enough time from the first creation to Adam for animals and humans to have lived and died a natural life. If there was violence some of them may have even died from other than natural causes. As far as the sin is concerned I believe the sin that is within us has been passed down from Adam. That is the sin the entire Bible refers to; the sin that is within modern man. The previous beings may have also developed sinful ways. We have a record they lived but do not have a record of their life. We do know Lucifer was cast out of Heaven before Adam was formed. His influence may have already taken hold. God's wish to save his newly formed man from their increasing violence is the reason He did not give Adam the knowledge of good and evil. Of course once that knowledge was introduced into us violence soon followed. It manifested itself first in Cain. The same violence that first appeared in modern man through Cain may have for years been developing in prehistoric man.

When God decided to destroy life on the Earth, He made the decision which animals would be saved. Chapter 6, verse 20 says the animals would come to Noah. *"Of fowls after their kind, and of cattle after their kind, of every creeping thing of the earth after his kind, two of every sort* **shall come** *into thee, to keep them alive"*. Chapter seven, verses 8 & 9 tells us the animals went into the ark to Noah. *"8Of clean beasts, and of beasts that are not clean, and of fowls, and of every thing that creepeth upon the earth, 9There went in two and two unto Noah into the ark, the male and the female, as God had commanded Noah"*. Noah did not go out and gather the animals as is commonly taught in children's Bible Stories. They came to Noah. The importance of that is the animals that came to the ark were the ones God chose to save; the animals of the second creation.

One argument that helps with the one creation teaching is the statement that two of every animal went into the ark. The Bible says, *"6:19And of every living thing of all flesh, two of every sort shalt thou bring into the ark, to keep them alive with tee; they shall be male and female."* This is commonly interpreted as being everything that was on the earth during the time before the flood. Of course that is making the assumption the same animals existed before and after the flood. That assumption comes from the fact the traditional Bible Story of Noah's Ark was being told well before dinosaur bones were discovered. It is time to change the story. What the verse actually refers to is everything that was on the earth at the time Moses was given the Word to record. The animals that Moses wrote about as going in two and two and being saved were the animals that were on the earth during his lifetime. These were the animals that were of the 'generations' of the Earth. He was not referring to the animals that were destroyed. Therefore, the statement is accurate even though not two of every animal that existed before the flood was saved on the ark.

This is difficult for most traditional religious teachers because they teach that the same animals that exist today have always existed. They ignore the fact that bones of an entire group of animals that do not still exist have been found. It is obvious these animals were not modern animals that simply became extinct over time. Even with the evidence in front of them, religious teachers have not searched for a biblical explanation. They have been taught that the term 'every' refers to all of the animals that God ever created and they teach the same. They do not want to change the story. I understand it is difficult to change in 150 years what had been taught for the previous 1500 years. We should not allow that to be an excuse. Look at how easy it was for scientist to change their teaching when Darwin published his unfounded theory based simply on unexplainable observations. With the discovery of the new bones religious leaders should have been just as curious to find a biblical answer as Darwin was to find any answer. But, as I said earlier, the pattern of religious education is just to teach what you have been taught.

Chapter 7, verse 15 tells us the animals that were saved were the ones wherein is the breath of life. *"And they went in unto Noah into the ark, two and two of all flesh, wherein is the breath of life."* These would be the animals of the second creation. The animals of the second creation were formed by God from the ground (2:19) just as Adam had been (2:7). While the Bible does not say so directly, it stands to reason that these animals would have received the breath of life from God after they were formed just as Adam had after he was formed. This is supported by verse 7:22. *"All in whose nostrils was the breath of life…"* The animals and man of the first creation were created, fully intact and alive, by God's words. The ground brought forth the living animals. Adam, the animals of the second creation, and Eve, because they were formed by GOD, needed to receive the breath of life from God to become living souls. This is another way the animals of the second creation would be distinguished from the animals of the first creation. The animals of chapter 2 would be the ones wherein is the breath of life and were saved on the Ark.

Traditionalists who do acknowledge the dinosaurs generally teach they died of after leaving the ark. I do not believe they ever entered the ark. We have to read carefully the verses that tell us which animals were and were not saved on the ark.

Chapter 7, verses 21-23, tell us what was destroyed in the flood. This passage must be studied carefully. "21*And all flesh died that moved upon the earth, both fowl, and of cattle, and of beast, and of every creeping thing that creepeth upon the earth, and every man: 22.All in whose nostrils was the breath of life, of all that was in the dry land died. 23.And every living substance was destroyed which was upon the face of the ground, both man, and cattle, and the creeping things, and the fowl of the heaven; and they were destroyed from the earth; and Noah only remained alive, and they that were with him in the ark*". Verses 22 and 23 separate the animals into two groups. One group is those in which was the breath of life. The other is every living substance. Verse 22 refers back to verse 21 which names the things with the breath of life that would be destroyed: fowl, cattle, beast, creeping thing, and man. Verse 23 specifies the things that were included in the category called substances that would be destroyed: man, cattle, creeping things, and fowl. The most important word in these verses is the word 'and' at the beginning of verse 23(KJV). The word 'and' tells us the organisms of verse 23 were in addition to those of verses 21 and 22. It indicates that even GOD viewed the animals he formed and breathed into the breath of life (chapter two), and the animals he spoke into creation (Chapter one) {substance} as two distinct groups. The word 'and' separates the creatures of verse 21 from those of verse 23. Those referred to as substances are the dinosaur and prehistoric man.

Other translations have changed the word 'and' to better suit their purposes or the commonly accepted explanation. Knowing that the KJV was translated from the original text (for the specific purpose of having an accurate English translation) it has been noted that certain words were added to increase understanding in the English language. These added words are usually printed in Italics. My copy of the Bible includes those italicized words. The word 'and' at the beginning of verse 23 is not in italics. This would indicate the word was needed for the literal translation. Therefore, the creatures of verse 23 would be in addition to the creatures of verse 22.

I want to remind you once again of the difference between the animals and man that were spoken into creation in chapter 1, and the animals and man that were formed in chapter two. In chapter 1 "God said" and created everything that was created at that time. They were created as living, breathing beings. There is no mention of the 'breath of life' being given to any of them. The animals were created **before** the species man. In chapter 2 man and the animals were both formed of the ground then the women from the man. The man was created first, then the animals, then the women. GOD breathed into the nostrils of man the breath of life in order for the man to become a living soul. It would stand to reason the animals that were formed (not spoken into existence) would also need the breath of life to become alive. Since they were created in the same fashion as Adam they would have had the same need for life. The woman, here, (Eve) was made from a living soul (Adam), but still she was formed by GOD. These differences would be the reason God referred to the men and animals of the second creation as those *"in whose nostrils is the breath of life"* (VS. 21-22) and the men and animals of the first creation as *"every living substance"* (VS. 23).

Chapter 7, verse 15 clearly states the animals that went into the ark to Noah were only those that were of the flesh that had the breath of life. *"And they went in unto Noah into the ark, two and two of all flesh, wherein is the breath of life"*. None of the animals that fell under the description of living substances (v. 23) went into the ark. This includes pre-historic man and dinosaurs. The remainder of the animals that had the breath of life (v.22) and all of the animals described as living substances (v.23) were destroyed. The animals mentioned in verse 23 as being destroyed, that were first called every living substance then were individually named, include the animals of the chapter one creation, that we have named dinosaurs. That is why, as science and the fossil records have shown, all of the dinosaurs died off suddenly. The meteor explanation, which I don't think is worth discussing, is another piece of creative fiction. The truth is the dinosaurs were not taken by God into the Ark to be saved and therefore died in the flood.

The bottom line here is that a Christian/Jewish person must believe God's created animals and man have always co-existed. Even if you think pre-historic man and dinosaurs were separated by time from modern man and animals, you have to believe man (whether pre-historic or modern) co-existed with the animals (whether dinosaur or modern). What I have tried to show here is that modern animals and man co-existed with the dinosaur and pre-historic man. There was a period of time from the second creation of earth's creatures to the great flood that all of God's creation co-existed. It was in the flood that all of the animals we call dinosaurs were killed along with pre-historic man and all other life that was not preserved aboard the ark.

# What About What Science Teaches?

Since the time of Charles Darwin there has been a dispute between creationists and evolutionists. Unfortunately in the realm of secular education the evolutionists have had the upper hand. Thanks to the separation of church and state granted by our constitution, along with various lawsuits and Supreme Court interpretations of the constitution, creation can not be taught in schools as the truth; only as an alternative to evolution or simply another theory. Even teaching it as a theory is difficult because the vast majority of the science textbooks discusses evolution in detail and will totally ignore or scarcely mention creation even as a theory. With the current interpretation of the laws, most teachers are afraid to open their Bible in the classroom. Then, the wording of the textbooks is usually such that it is evident the writers want evolution to be taken as the truth. This has created a situation where even though evolution is called a theory in the textbooks it is taken as fact. To make matters worse, the majority of science teachers believe evolution to be the truth. That includes teachers who claim to be Christian.

Although evolution is officially called a theory, and scientists as well as science teachers know this, it is most often taught as fact. In the classroom there is seldom any mention of the true fact that most of the information being taught about the evidence for evolution is pure speculation. The discovery of the bones of extinct animals spurned speculation, which turned into hypothesis, which turned into theories, which were then taught without any scientific proof. The information that is often given as proof is nothing more than creative thinking.

The problem with the process when it comes to evolution is how the theories were formed. Within the scientific method the usual process is that theories are formed only after a hypothesis has been repeatedly tested with consistent results. The theory of evolution, however, was accepted simply because there was not another explanation for the existence of these extinct animals at the time the theory was introduced by Darwin. The discovery of these bones, along with Darwin's observations, created a deep curiosity among the people. Once Darwin put his thoughts in a book people took his ideas as fact although there was not, and has never been, any true evidence supporting his statements. However, the religious community and its traditional one creation teaching did not, and still does not, have a plausible counter explanation to offer. When Darwin presented his theory it immediately quenched the people's thirst for an answer. Therefore it was accepted and taken as fact.

It has been my pleasure to find that recent scientific advances have shown evolution could not stand up to the tests. Of course only the open minded scientists have admitted this openly. I will discuss that in more detail later.

One important component for explaining the age of dinosaur bones in terms of millions of years is the elaborate explanation scientists have concocted for how the bones were buried. The say over long periods of time the bones were covered by sediment and buried deeper and deeper under layers of soil. As time continued the processes reversed themselves and slowly uncovered the bones. In other words the same processes that buried the bones unburied the bones. Then there are the bones that are said to have been buried in river beds, and over time the rivers dried up. If it happens to be near a current river, scientists will say the river has changed its course. At any rate, any and all of the explanations given would take millions of years to occur through what we see as natural processes. That became the time frame scientists wanted so they devised methods that would give that time frame and fit their theories.

Now I will do something scientists hate; state the obvious truth. The explanation of why the skeletons of dinosaurs were buried is pretty simple. They sank in, and were covered by, the mud caused by the great flood. That is the same reason entire ancient cities have been found buried. That is also why the majority of the areas where the bones are found show signs they were once covered by water. They were. The layers that scientists are so proud to point out would have been created by the mud along with the suspended sediment that would settle out of the water as it calmed and the silt left behind as the waters receded and dried up. This explanation may seem too simple by scientific standards. Scientists want every process which took place on the earth to have been something complicated. Christian scientists should use the Bible as one of their primary resources when they are searching for answers. They could then use their scientific knowledge to verify the truth.

There are a couple of other reasons scientists will not accept that explanation. First, scientists will not admit the cities and dinosaurs were buried at the same time because they do not want to believe dinosaurs and humans co-existed. They teach that the dinosaurs were extinct millions of years before humans developed. How long would it have taken for the cities to be buried under the process scientists describe? Second, this explanation does not allow for the even more millions of years it would take for the process of the dinosaur's bones to be buried then resurface according to scientist's common explanations. They really want the 'millions-of-years' theory to be true. Besides that, it is not an explanation that requires scientific discovery. Of course they could spend their effort validating the truth rather than trying to validate speculation.

Simple explanations such as the great flood do not give scientists much to do. They want all explanations to be difficult so they will have reasons to do research. They also want to be able to claim discovery. In order to accomplish these things, scientists will often devise research methods that are justified by their difficult explanations. In other words, they set out to prove themselves right, not necessarily find the truth. They want their theories of millions of years of evolution to be true, so they devised a test that would give the results that would support their theories; radiometric dating. The primary difficulty I have with that method is there is no way to know if radiometric dating is accurate without knowing the precise composition of what they claim to be the ancient atmosphere. They do not know the composition of that ancient atmosphere, and know they do not know. They make up what they want the composition of the atmosphere to be so their dating system will give the results they want. Scientists have even admitted there has to be adjustments in their calculations to compensate for inaccuracies. They create data and adjust their own methods and formulas to get the results they want. They refuse to accept the obvious.

Scientists also have devised theories to explain why there is what they call a gap in the fossil record. Of course once again there is no proof, or even the smallest amount of evidence, any of their explanations are true. The truth is there has never been any evidence found that truely shows a gradual evolution of any species. The fact that the Bible has a record of two different acts of creation of man and animals explains the differences in the fossils that have been found. The evolutionary gap scientists are trying to fill can not be filled. It does not exist. That is, it does not exist in the evolutionary form they try to claim. There was no evolution from the first creation to the second, although there may have been some mixing of the two gene pools (ex. Cain, his wife, and their offspring). That would account for the differences between Neanderthal and Cro-Magnon people. The mixing of the gene pools, not long time evolution, created the differences. Of course that is assuming the scientist's claim that there is a difference between the two is accurate. Do we find the same types of differences among human groups today (Pigmies, Chinese, Aborigines)? Just as there is no evolution of humans, there also is no evolution of animals from one species to another (pre-historic primate to apes and man). There is no gap, just a restart.

One thing scientists have discovered is that the skeletons of snakes have remnants of legs. Evolutionary scientists have claimed that discovery to be evidence of evolution. If that is to be taken as scientific evidence, it would seem to me to be evidence snakes were in fact de-evolving. In other instances scientists claim creatures that swam, over time, evolved by developing the ability to crawl out of the water, then through continued evolution developed legs and walked. At the same time they want us to believe the snake's evolution was in the opposite direction. An animal that once walked on legs evolve into one that would slither. The ability to walk on legs would have been an advantage over not having legs. According to the survival of the fittest portion of their theory this reverse evolution should have never happened. Once again they changed their explanation to make the situation fit their theory.

The truth of this phenomenon is found in Genesis, chapter 3 verse 14, *"And the Lord God said unto the serpent, Because thou hast done this, thou art cursed above all cattle, and above every beast of the field; upon thy belly shalt thou go, and dust shalt thou eat all the days of thy life."* God gave Moses these words to record thousands of years before scientists made their discovery. The actual event as it was recorded took place an unknown number of years before Moses. The scientist's discovery has simply verified the truth of the Bible. They won't admit that because it doesn't fit their evolutionary theory. To say the truth of the Bible explains the existence of the leg remnants is too simple of an answer for scientists. The problem here is when man first decides what the answer is he wants to find he will create a way for that answer to be found. Even when he knows the truth, if it does not fit the answer he wants, he will ignore that truth. Most scientists probably heard the explanation of the snake's leg remnants as children in church but will ignore it because they do not see it as science. Every truth, to them, has to be explainable through man's science.

God could have totally removed the legs with no evidence they ever existed. The reason He left those remnants is so that through discovery we would know His Word is the truth. Because science has revealed something that would otherwise have gone un-noticed we can now know the story of the serpent as recorded by Moses is true. As I stated earlier, the historic portion of the Bible is complete to the point that it will give us the answers to everything we observe in this world. The leg remnants on the snake skeletons have been observed. The Bible gives us the explanation of what has been observed. In this case the scientist's discovery also proves the truth of the Bible. Remember, the Bible was written well before the scientist's discovery. Why scientists who say they are Christian do not look to the Word of God for answers is puzzling to me. Also, why do they not use the knowledge they have gained to verify the truth of the Bible? After all it is from God that we get true knowledge. "*That is every thing ye are enriched by Him, in all utterance, and in all knowledge.*" (1 Corinthians 1:5)

In their efforts to have their evolutionary theories accepted as truths, scientists have created radiometric dating. It is the only way they are able to get their desired results when trying to find the age of fossils to be in the millions of years. Although different radioactive isotopes are used to measure years in the millions, the radioactive isotope that is most commonly known by the average man is carbon-14. The dating method involves measuring the ratio of carbon-14 to cabon-12 (the naturally occurring isotope of carbon) in living organisms and comparing it to the same ratio in fossils. This method (using carbon-14) is said to be accurate only up to 50,000 years. Carbon-14 has the shortest half-life of the long-lived radioactive isotopes. Since, as a Christian, I do not believe in the millions-of-years theories anyway, I feel it is appropriate to use carbon-14 for this discussion.

The half-life of a radioactive isotope is the amount of time scientists say it would take for half of a lot of the isotope to decay back to a non-radioactive daughter isotope. They say only half of the lot will decay within that time given period. Then half of the remaining lot will decay within the same amount of time; then half of the remaining; and so on.

What is radiometric, or carbon-14, dating? To put it simply, the scientist will measure the ratio of carbon-14 (a radioactive isotope) to carbon-12 (the naturally occurring isotope) in the remains of a previously living organism. They compare this ratio to what they feel the original ratio of the carbon isotopes consumed by living organisms should have been; based on the amount of carbon-14 that is produced in the atmosphere from nitrogen-14 by particles of light rays, and the amount of carbon-12 that occurs naturally. Using mathematical calculations, and what they say is the half-life of carbon-14, they claim to be able to figure how long it would take for a lot of carbon-14 to decay back to the original nitrogin-14. Given the two measured ratios, they say they are able to place an age on a fossil.

Radiometric dating wasn't fully developed in the early 1960's. Since that time advances have been made and scientists have accepted the results they have gotten for the ages of rocks and fossils as reliable. While they make that statement they admit the process is not perfect and is still being refined. In other words they are still trying to get it to do what they want it to do.

The problem with radiometric dating is that before the results of this method can be objectively accepted as accurate certain assumptions have to be made. My question is how can you claim the method to be true is if you have to assume certain un-provable information?

> 1) You must assume carbon-14 decays at a constant rate; that rate has not changed over time; and the rate is not affected by unknown factors.
> 2) You must assume the amount of carbon-14 that was produced and the amount that was absorbed by the specimen being tested (through consumption) is known for the time period in which the specimen lived.
> 3) You must assume the ratio of carbon-14 to carbon-12 in living organisms has not changed over time.
> 4) You must assume carbon-14 does not start to decay while in living organisms.

5) You must assume nitrogen-14 (the daughter isotope of carbon-14) was not present in the specimen at the time of its death.

6) You must assume nitrogen-14 is not absorbed by living organisms (naturally or through consumption) and could not have entered the fossil specimen by any means other than carbon-14 decay (either while alive or dead).

If any one, or all, of these statements can not be taken from a statement of assumption to a statement of certainty then carbon-14 dating can not be proven to be accurate. In a truly scientific method nothing should be left to assumptions. I do not think scientists can say without making assumptions that they know with certainty any of these things about carbon-14 or any other radioactive isotope.

Scientists claim to know the rate of decay of certain radioactive isotopes. Without knowing why only half of a lot would decay over the period of time, and not having observed a lot for the entire period of time (most half lives are said to be in the thousands of years), scientists could not know if their computations of half lives are accurate. They also could not know if the rate of decay is truly constant. The only thing they can know for sure is how long it takes for the process to begin.

There are problems or inconsistencies with each of the assumptions concerning carbon-14 dating. Carbon-14 decays into nitrogen-14. Scientists claim the decay rate of carbon-14 is a half-life of 5730 years and is constant. That is saying half an amount of carbon-14 will convert back to nitrogen-14 in 5730 years (plus or minus 40 years). To put it simply if you have a lot of 1000 parts of carbon-14 then after 5730 years 500 parts will decay back to nitrogen-14. Seems to me if you have 1000 parts of carbon-14 and in 5730 years it has decayed to 500 parts, then the last 500 parts should decay in the next 5730 years. Therefore, if any sample has any detectable carbon-14 then it has to be less than 11,460 years old. Of course scientists say only half of the 500 parts will decay in the next 5730 years. If only 250 parts would decay in the second 5730 years (and so forth) then the decay rate is in fact variable and is based on the amount of existing carbon-14. When you look at pure numbers the rate of decay actually decreases as the years pass. Scientists put the rate in terms of a percentage (50% per time period).

If it is true the number of carbon-14 atoms that will actually decay within a half-life depends directly on the original number, there must be some other factor that affects the decay rate. This must also be true for the simple fact that all of the carbon-14 that exists in an organism at the time of its death does not all decay back to nitrogen-14 at the same time. If one molecule of the isotope decays why wouldn't another? One of these factors could be either exposure or non-exposure. Given a certain quantity, the larger the amount of atoms that are in a defined space, the larger the number of exposed or unexposed atoms, thus the larger the number of atoms that decay. As the number of atoms within that same space is reduced the number of exposed or unexposed atoms is reduced, thus reducing the number of atoms that decay. This could possibly explain why all of the carbon-14 atoms do not all decay at the same time. Thus the rate of decay will not be constant.

If the rate of decay in the dead organism has anything to do with when the isotope was consumed while the organism was alive then the scientists would have to know the exact diet of the organism. They would actually need to know the last few meals the organism ate. There is no way they could possibly know this information. Scientists can not explain why the entire lot of the isotope does not decay at the same time.

Why does carbon-14 not begin to decay in living organisms? (Or does it?) If a process that occurs during life slows or prevents the decay, then other processes in fact do affect the decay rate. When that protection from decay is removed at the point death of the organism all of the carbon-14 should begin to decay at the same time. If all of it does not start to decay at the same time exposure or the lack of exposure must be the underlying factor. As more of the carbon-14 is exposed as the dead organism decomposes the rate of carbon-14 decay would increase. Therefore, the fossils of organisms, that have been dead for a given period of time, would test much older than they really are. If exposure or some other process, does not affect the rate of decay, then that brings back the question, why does all of the carbon-14 in a dead organism not decay at the same time?

If the entire lot of the isotope does start to decay at the same time and scientists think otherwise then it would be easy to get the long periods of time they want. They say the half-life of carbon-14 is 5730 years although they have not had a lot of the isotope for that period of time. If an organism dies and the process of decay begins immediately, then by the time it is tested it may have only a small amount of the isotope left and would test to be much older than it actually was. That discrepancy would take place simply because the tester would have certain expectations based on the supposed half-life of the isotope. I believe this is what gives the scientists the measures of millions of years when they test the dinosaur bones. Although they have not had a lot of any radioactive isotope that is used for dating for the period of a half-life they have set their expectations based on their estimates of that half-life.

Has the ratio of carbon-14/carbon-12 been the same

throughout history? No. In fact it has not been constant in recent history. During the era when massive amounts of fossil fuels were burned there was a lot of carbon dioxide released into the air that was depleted in carbon-14. In other words carbon 12 was being produced at a rate that was higher than normal. Because the ratio of carbon-14 to carbon-12 would have been immediately affected, organisms that died during that time period would, by the radiometric dating method, automatically test older than they are. Biblically, the pre-flood atmosphere would not have had as much carbon-14 as today's atmosphere. The cloud cover of the pre-flood time would not have allowed as many cosmic rays to penetrate the atmosphere. Therefore, not as much carbon-14 would have been produced. Comparing the ratio of carbon isotopes from today to the same isotopes in organisms from that time would naturally cause them to test older than they are.

When discussing the cycle of carbon-14 from the atmosphere to plants to animals, evolutionary scientists have said the ratio is constant. But, there is scientific evidence that plants discriminate against carbon dioxide containing carbon-14. That is, they take up less than would be expected and thus test older than they really are. Furthermore, different types of plants discriminate differently. This would cause plants that lived at the same time to test differently using this method. Of course different animals eat different plants. How much difference will that make? Since carbon-14 is not the naturally occurring form of carbon, do the animals also automatically discriminate against that particular isotope? That is, does the animal body metabolize the different isotopes of carbon differently? If so, that would be another factor that would have an immediate affect on the results. Would the organisms metabolize and store the two isotopes at the same rate? How many other questions could be asked?

Evidence that the organisms do not use and store the two

isotopes at the same rate was shown in a musk ox that was found in Alaska. When different parts of the animal were tested for age, very different dates were the result. I just said this may be the result of how the organism uses and stores carbon. I could be wrong. It also could have been the result of different parts of the dead animal being exposed to the elements at different times and for different amounts of time. At any rate it definitely demonstrates that the rate of decay is not constant. Scientists do not want to address these types of issues. If it is shown that their method of age determination is inaccurate, the so called proof of their theory is out the window. If there are anomalies within one animal, just how inaccurate must the radiometric dating method be?

There are other examples of why carbon-14 dating is not accurate. For each case where there are inaccuracies the scientists will simple re-calibrate to achieve the answers they want. When re-calibration does not give the desired results, they will change to another set of radioactive isotopes. As I said earlier, I used the carbon isotopes as my example because they are the ones most widely known by the general public from grade school education. Other isotopes are said to be used for older fossils. No matter which isotopes are used there are certain un-provable assumptions that have to be made and accepted such as: the starting conditions and ratios are known; decay rates have always been constant; the ratio of parent to daughter isotopes has always been the same where no isotopes were lost or added. Just taking into account the first assumption, there is no way scientists could possibly know the ratios of the isotopes at the time the ancient organism lived. This is especially true if you believe their millions-of-years theories.

As I stated I've used carbon-14 for this discussion because that is what is used in most textbooks and I felt most people could identify with it. But, to stress my point more clearly I will briefly touch on other aspects of radiometric dating and other isotopes.

Scientists admit that in order to get the results they want they sometimes have to use different combinations of isotopes. The scientists that are considered specialists in selecting the method to be used are called Geochronologists. Their primary job is to select the method that will be applied to the particular aging problem they are trying to solve. They claim to be able to design the experiment in such a way that the results can be checked for reliability. It would seem to me that the two steps of selecting the method and designing the experiment indicates they are selecting and designing a way to get the results they want, not the truth. If the radiometric methods were truly accurate there would be not reason to change the combination of isotopes used or redesign the experiment. The same method should work with any fossil or rock being tested. Scientists explain the need for different methods by the differences in the half-lives of the various isotopes and whether the specimen being test was taken from an open or closed system. The later portion of that statement shows that exposure must affect the rates of decay of the isotope, and they know that.

One of the three principal methods use for dating is the potassium-40 isotope which decays to argon-40. Even reading the scientist's explanation of this method brings into view several problems. Potassium-40 actually decays into two different isotopes, argon-40 and calcium-40. They claim to know the ratio of potassium atoms that would decay to each new atom but says calcium is too abundant to use for dating. If they truly accurately knew the ratio they should be able to use either argon or calcium. Argon escapes easily from the specimen if it is heated. Scientists could not know the temperature change the specimen may have gone through over the years. There has to be corrections made during analysis for the argon from the atmosphere that is naturally present in most minerals. Are they corrections or adjustments to get the answers they want? The specimen must not have gained or lost any potassium or argon naturally. Scientists can not possibly know this. There are too many things that could easily create inaccuracies for this method to be considered reliable.

There are also problems with the method that uses rubidium-87 which decays to strontium-87, the second of the three principal methods. Rubidium is claimed to have a half-life of 48.8 billion years. How could scientists ever have a sample that they can say half of the sample has decayed? Both rubidium and strontium occur as trace elements in rocks so all rocks should test as being young. To get around that problem they only test samples that are high in rubidium and low in initial strontium, which means they can not prove any decay had taken place. How could they know the amount of intial strontium? That makes this method not very useful since most samples have significant amounts of strontium. With all of these issues scientists have to compensate or adjust the results. In other words they make the results be what they want them to be.

The Uranium to Lead method, the third primary method, is just as flawed if not more so. Without discussing the series of isotopes that the sample of uranium decays through before becoming lead, and the changing ratios over time, when the scientists admit corrections have to be made for the initial amount of lead in the sample it is easy to see this method could not possibly be accurate. How could they be sure how much lead was originally in a sample that is thousands or millions of years old (by their measure)?

It should be easy to see that no matter which method of radiometric dating is used certain assumptions have to be made. It is impossible for scientists to know all of the information they would actually need to state emphatically that any one method is truly accurate. They have never had a sample of any of the radioactive elements for a half-life to say their estimations are accurate. They could not possibly know how much of an element existed at the time a specimen died. This is especially true if they believe their own statements that millions of years have passed and that the atmosphere has changed over time. The problem here is that with these and other assumptions that have been mentioned the very definition of good science is contradicted.

My discussion of radiometric dating is to support my previous statement that scientists decided what they wanted the answers to be (millions of years), then devised various methods to make their predictions true. Their results, however are not accurate and only lend to perpetuate the evolutionary theories. In fact, creationist researchers have suggested that radiometric dates of 35,000-40,000 years (which would fall within the parameters of carbon dating) should be re-calibrated to the biblical dates of the flood. I agree with that. These dates can be figured by simply doing a chronology of the Bible from the time of the flood to the present. It is also my opinion that the older radiometric dates should be re-calibrated to the biblical dates of the first creation (the beginning) and the second creation to just before the flood. I don't know how much time passed between the first and second creations but it was not millions of years.

# What Does Modern Scientific Research Show?

It has truly been a pleasure to find out that objective scientists have, over the last few decades, admitted evolution, as it is commonly taught, could not possibly be true. Modern scientific discoveries and increased knowledge about the complexities of living organisms has shown that spontaneous generation, or an accidental beginning of life, is not possible. Furthermore these same advances in knowledge gives support to the idea of creation by intelligent design, or more to the point, a spiritual being; God. Science not only disproves evolution of species and supports creation by God, it also supports the idea I have proposed here of the two separate creations of Earth's creatures.

When Darwin first stated his theory of evolution he had no way of knowing what the evidence would really reveal. He used data he had collected from pure observation and made assumptions about the things he had observed. He and the scientists of his day could not have imagined the complexities of living organisms that would be discovered over the next century and a half. Darwin knew there were gaps in the known fossil record of his time but thought future discoveries would fill the gaps. He also thought future discoveries would show how complex organs could have developed through slight modifications of simpler organs over long periods of time. He admitted in his book Origin of Species that if these things could not be demonstrated his theory would not hold up. Unfortunately his theory has held up despite the fact the gaps has not been filled and it has been demonstrated that complex organs and organisms did not and could not have developed by slight modifications over time.

We could discuss the many fallacies of Darwin's theory of evolution but for this project I am primarily concerned with the gap in the fossil record. Science has shown that the organisms which appeared on the modern side of the gap did not evolve from previous organisms but appeared suddenly and fully formed. This sudden influx of new species into the living world has been named the Cambrian Explosion. Even with the many new archeological discoveries over the past century, of previously unknown species, there has never been a discovery of any transitional species between the creatures that existed before the explosion and after. This absence of transitional forms is one of the main reasons objective scientists have dismissed the theory of evolution and see it only as a myth. In fact, the gap between the pre-Cambrian and post-Cambrian fossils is so large nothing can really be said that would show any connection through evolutionary ancestry. The animals of the two time periods are not biologically related in any way. It has recently been shown that the DNA samples from the two time periods has absolutely nothing in common. This is scientific evidence of my belief in the two creature creations.

There have been numerous books written that show the theory of evolution can not be supported by true scientific research. There are also a number of books that express the thought that the more we understand about life and the universe, the more we realize there has to be an intelligent creator responsible for it all. I have also read several articles where scientific discoveries have been supported by biblical passages and biblical teachings have been verified by scientific discoveries. Because I have been a believer in God from an early age and a lover of science since elementary school, I have always felt religion and science should be able to support each other. I believe the fossil record with its gap and the Cambrian Explosion help to explain chapter two of Genesis as being a description of God forming a new group of creatures as apposed to the chapter being a re-statement of chapter one.

One thing that I would like to point out is that I have never read or heard any discussion about any of the dinosaurs evolving into new species. The fossil record shows that they did in fact live a long time ago. It also shows that they all died off suddenly. Another thing the fossil record does not show is any species that evolved into the dinosaurs. Just as there is no record of any transition forms leading to the organisms that appeared after the Cambrian Explosion, there is no record of transition forms leading to the dinosaurs. The gap in the fossil record itself testifies to the fact there was no evolution between the two. The lack of evolutionary evidence leading to the dinosaurs and leading to the post Cambrian organisms verifies both sets of organisms appeared in their original form and independently of each other.

One thing that modern science is finally admitting is that much of the evidence that has been used in the past to support the teaching of evolution has been faked or, at the least, extremely exaggerated. The *archaeoraptor* fossil was publicized as being the missing link between birds and dinosaurs. It, in fact, was found to be two different fossils glued together by the very scientist who was making the claim. DNA that scientists at one point claimed to have found in sixty-five million year old dinosaur bones turned out to be turkey DNA. The famous depiction of Java man (ape man with a sloping forehead, receding chin, jutting jaw, and heavy brow) is nothing more than an artist's rendering created from the discovery of a skullcap, three teeth, and a femur. It was later admitted the femur did not go with the skullcap, and the skullcap was within the range of modern humans. The drawings of embryos by Ernst Haeckel which were intended to show that the similarities between the embryos pointed toward a common ancestor were manipulated to look more similar than they really were. Even before that, he had deliberately chosen embryos that would come closest to fitting his preconceived idea. The more the truth is revealed, the more it becomes evident the evolutionary gap can not be filled. In fact, evolution as a whole can not be supported. If Haeckel had been looking for the truth he may have realized the similarities point toward a common Creator.

Modern understanding of biological functioning of organisms has shown that evolution could not possibly explain the complexity of the operations that take place in organisms, organ systems, organs, tissues, or even individual cells. Because in most cases the entire system has to be intact to function, it would have been impossible for the system to evolve one component at a time. A single component or a non-functioning system would have been selected for extinction according to the laws of natural selection as explained in evolutionary theory. More to the point, a system could not have evolved at all if it was not already functioning. In order for any organ to evolve, the organism would have to have first developed a concept of the functioning of the organ and a need for that function.

A good example of such a system is the eye. A common sense view of the theories of spontaneous generation or accidental life and evolution should show that if the first organisms did not have sight, there would have been no concept of sight. Therefore, there would not have been a need for any organism to develop the eye. Setting that realism aside, if an organism did happen to develop one component of the eye, and not the whole eye, that component would have been useless. Natural selection, according to the usual teaching, would have caused that useless component to disappear from successive generations of that organism. If another component happened to evolve it also would have been useless without the whole eye. No single component of the eye functions to allow sight without the functioning of all of the components. This is realized whenever a person loses the function of one of the components of the eye. Blindness occurs. According to the laws of natural selection, as they are taught, the eye could never have evolved unless it suddenly appeared fully intact and functioning as an organ within an organism. But, that would not be evolution would it?

Organisms that existed before the Cambrian Explosion were completely intact and functioning. There is absolutely no scientific evidence and, thus, no scientific reason to say the dinosaurs evolved from a lower form of life. That idea was simply a creation from the imagination of a person with limited knowledge, Darwin. The myth has been perpetuated by those who wanted a simple explanation for the existence of the dinosaurs that did not include God. It has not mattered that there has never been any true evidence to support any of the claims. They were/are happy with the feeling that in living their life they did not have to be accountable to a higher power. The prolonged teaching of this falsehood has also been aided by the fact those who do believe in God have not offered a biblical explanation that includes the dinosaur and scientific discoveries to refute the scientist's evolutionary claims.

The science of archeology has shown that the organisms that came into existence at the Cambrian Explosion appeared suddenly, completely intact, and functioning. Even though the appearance of these new organisms is something for which there is much evidence, it does not bother the evolutionists much because the creationists still do not offer a biblical explanation. The lack of a biblical explanation has left the evolutionists the opportunity to claim evidence would eventually be found that would bridge the gap. That has not happened. In fact, as more knowledge has been gained, it has become more evident the gap between the organisms that existed before the Cambrian Explosion and after can not be bridged. The evidence shows that the organisms which came into existence at the Cambrian Explosion are in no way related to the organisms which existed before.

Adam was not the first human. He was the first being of the Cambrian explosion. The other animals of the post-Cambrian are the ones formed in Genesis 2:19. The pre-Cambrian organism are those spoken into existence and recorded in Genesis one. The dinosaurs are pre-Cambrian. Modern animals are post-Cambrian.

# Bringing It All Together

For as much time as I am aware, science and religion have operated as two distinctly different institutions. For the most part they each have claimed to be right while saying the other is wrong. As things happen in God's time, we are finally getting to the point that the two disciplines are coming together. Each has finally admitted the other may not be totally off base. Continued gains in scientific knowledge have led a large portion of the scientific community to admit that Creation is a much more realistic explanation for why the universe and life exists than is the Big Bang and Spontaneous Generation. Likewise, religious leaders have come to realize the laws of physics and other scientific claims are also the truth and can, as a matter of fact, be used to prove some of the statements and events in the Bible are the truth. The objective application of advances in scientific knowledge will soon be able to verify the statement, "In the beginning God created the heavens and the earth."

The two disciplines will never be able to totally come together until they each let go of some of the things that keep them apart. The subject I have been discussing in this project, the two creation events, is one area the two could come together. Science needs to give up the spontaneous generation and evolution teaching, and religion needs to give up the one creation teaching. I have shown that the Bible teaches two different creations (chapters 1 & 2 of Genesis). I have also shown where science verifies the two creations (the pre and post Cambrian organisms) and disproves evolution.

Let me summarize the information I have discussed.

The creation of the heavens and the earth, and the arrangement of the Earth, happened only once. There is no repeated account of this in chapter two. This account is given in Chapter 1, verses 1-19. Verse 1 says, *"In the beginning God created the heavens and the earth."* This is probably the most important verse that gives meaning to our existence. Without God in the picture we are just an accident and our existence has no purpose.

I did not address one topic in the section on science because it did not directly relate to the dinosaurs, but I think it is important to recognize that the sciences of cosmology and astronomy have determined that the universe definitely had a beginning. This is important because that is another area where science verifies the truth of the Bible. The cosmological argument first starts with the statement that whatever begins to exist has a cause. Scientific study and research of the stars have shown that there was a point in time that the universe came into existence. Most scientists still refer to that point in time as the Big Bang. (The term is not always used in relation to evolution.) Since there was a beginning to the existence of the universe, then it must be concluded that the universe has a cause. That cause is stated in the first verse of the Bible. That cause is God. Modern science is no longer in conflict with that statement, but instead supports it.

The creation of Earth's creatures is the primary focus of this project; more specifically the creation of the dinosaur. Since we (Believers) do believe God purposefully created the earth and all of the inhabitants thereof, and we know the dinosaurs once existed, we must also believe God purposefully created the dinosaurs. The topic that is most often avoided by both the religious and scientific communities is what the Bible says about this specific part of God's creation. The religious avoids the topic because when they say the creature creation started with the creation of Adam they can not account for the dinosaurs. The few who have tried to address the topic generally incorporates more science than Bible. The evolutionary scientists avoid the topic because to say the Bible mentions the creation of the dinosaurs does not leave room for their theory of evolution.

As I have repeated several times, I believe the Bible tells us the creation of the creatures that would inhabit the Earth happened twice as follows.

## CHAPTER 1

Vs. 20-23) GOD **said**; and created sea creatures and birds (together). Some scientists have tried to link pre-historic birds to reptiles. They may not be too far off seeing as they were created together. The similarities are not attributed to evolution however. They are attributed to the Creator. The primary focus here should be the other animals the birds were created with in chapter 1; the sea creatures. This was the day before the land animals would be created. The fowls created here were the pterodactyls and other flying dinosaurs.

Vs. 24-25) GOD **said**; and created land animals. The method of creation, God speaking them into existence, and the order of creation, before man, are the important points to be noticed here. These animals are the ones we call dinosaurs. They were brought forth from the ground by the words of God, not formed.

Vs. 26-28) God **said**; and created the species man (male and female together). GOD gave man dominion over the fish and animals that had already been created. Man and woman were created at the same time here. There is no indication one was created then the other from the first as with Adam and Eve in chapter two. This man and woman were not Adam and Eve. This species man are the ones we call pre-historic (Neanderthal and Cro-Magnon).

Note again the order of the account of creation of the creatures in chapter one. First the fowls were created along with the sea creatures (day five), then the land animals (the first part of day six), then the species man {male and female}(the last part of day six). Remember, this order can not be changed or refuted because it was established by the statement of days and how God was pleased after each step in the process. They were all spoken into existence.

## CHAPTER 2

Vs. 7) GOD **formed** man and breathed life into him. Adam was created by himself and was not simply spoken into existence as the species man had been in chapter one. He was also formed before any other land creatures in chapter two. The reason was given that there was not anyone to till the ground. He was placed alone in a garden God planted with plants He created before they were in the ground. (2:4)

Vs. 18) GOD **formed** land animals and birds out of the ground for the reason that Adam was alone. Unlike chapter one, the birds were formed with the land animals not the sea creatures. The sea creatures weren't re-created. The reason God formed these creatures was given. Therefore, the order of Adam being formed before these creatures can not be changed. This act of formation of these new creatures is the scientifically historical event scientists have named The Cambrian Explosion. Just as science has shown, there was no evolution from the animals and man first created in chapter one to these new animals and man. They were formed fully intact and became living souls by God's own breathe.

Vs. 21-22) GOD **made** woman (Eve) because the animals that were created to be a helper to Adam were still not comparable to him. Again, the reason that was given for Eve's creation clearly establishes her creation as being after the land animals. She was not created with the man as in chapter one. She was, however, formed from the male.

Note again the order of the account of the formation of the creatures in chapter two. First the man was formed for the reason there was no one till the ground. Then by reason he was alone the land animals were formed. By reason they were not comparable to Adam the woman was formed last. The sea creatures which would not die in the flood and thus would not be instrumental in the future development of the earth were not formed new in chapter two. They were not named as part of the "...*generations of the heavens and of the earth...*"(2:4)

I stress the differences of the order of the two accounts of the creations of Earth's creatures to make the point that since the two accounts are different, then the creatures of chapter one must be different from the creatures of chapter two. Further more, all of the creatures of chapter one were spoken into existence while all of the creatures of chapter two were formed from the ground (Eve from Adam). The land animals that were created in chapter one are the animals we call dinosaurs. The animals that were formed in chapter two are the modern animals. Although they probably didn't realize it and may not admit it, scientists have verified the second creation by the fossil record. They have named the second creation The Cambrian Explosion. The Cambrian Explosion began with the formation of Adam.

Evolutionary scientists will disagree with this because they do not want the dinosaurs and man to have lived during the same period of time. Religious scholars will disagree with this because they want Adam and Eve to be the first man and woman, and for there to have been only one creation. You can not believe in the Bible and say man and dinosaurs did not live during the same period of time, unless you say there is more to Earth's history than the Bible tells us. That is what the religious 'gap' believers teach. I believe the Bible gives us the history of the Earth from the beginning. Moreover, I believe the Bible Shows us there were creatures, including humans, created before Adam and Eve. In both accounts, chapter one and chapter two, man and animals co-existed. God gave man dominion over the animals in chapter one. Adam was given the task of naming the animals in chapter two. Therefore, much to the scientist's dismay, man and dinosaurs had to co-exist.

The differences of the chronological events of creation between chapter one and chapter two does not allow chapter two to be a restatement of chapter one or day six. That also does not allow Adam to be the first man created as religious scholars continue to teach.

In conclusion I will say GOD has given us the truth in His written Word. Man has decided for himself how the story should be told. When you read it again don't look for what you want it to be or what you have been taught. Read the truth the way it was given to Moses by God to be recorded. The animals we have come to call dinosaurs and the men we have given various names (but use the general term pre-historic) were created in the acts described in Genesis, Chapter one and designated by days. Modern man and modern animals were formed (The Cambrian

Explosion) in the acts described in Genesis, Chapter two and designated by God's reasons. The destruction that destroyed the animals of chapter one and most of the animals of chapter two was the great flood of Genesis; Chapters six through eight. All of the dinosaurs and pre-historic men, who were described as substances, were destroyed in the flood. Only the animals and man that were of the generations of the earth were saved aboard the ark. These would be the ones that became living souls by the breath of life from God. They are the modern animals we see today which were formed in chapter two and the unchanged line of Adam through Seth (the first child of Adam's generations) and Noah. The line of Cain was changed because he inter-married with the people of the spoken creation.

This is the truth I believe is written in the Word of God and verified by modern scientific discoveries. The first verse of the Bible describes the beginning of this physical universe's existence. I do not know how long God allowed the creatures of chapter one to exist before He formed the creatures of chapter two, however, these were two different groups of creatures. Modern animals are the Cambrian Explosion described in the verses of chapter two of Genesis. **The dinosaurs are the animals that were spoken into existence in chapter one of Genesis.**

**You Now Have A Biblical Explanation For The Existence Of The Dinosaurs.** Do not believe it because I said it. Believe it because God's Word, the Bible, says it.